CLAIMING GOD
RECLAIMING DIGNITY

CLAIMING GOD RECLAIMING DIGNITY

AFRICAN AMERICAN PASTORAL CARE

EDWARD P. WIMBERLY

Abingdon Press
Nashville

CLAIMING GOD: RECLAIMING DIGNITY
AFRICAN AMERICAN PASTORAL CARE

Copyright © 2003 by Abingdon Press

All rights reserved.

This book is printed on acid-free paper.

Library of Congress Cataloging-in-Publication Data

Wimberly, Edward P., 1943-
  Claiming God : reclaiming dignity—African American pastoral care / Edward P. Wimberly.
    p. cm.
  ISBN 0-687-03053-6 (pbk. : alk. paper)
  1. Pastoral care. 2. Interpersonal relations—Religious aspects—Christianity. 3. African Americans—Religion. I. Title.

BV4011.3 .W56 2003
253' .089'96073—dc21

2002153084

All scripture quotations unless noted otherwise are taken from the *New Revised Standard Version* of the Bible, copyright 1989 by the Division of Christian Education of the National Council of the Churches of Christ in the United States of America. Used by permission. All rights reserved.

03 04 05 06 07 08 09 10 11 12—10 9 8 7 6 5 4 3 2 1

MANUFACTURED IN THE UNITED STATES OF AMERICA

CONTENTS

PREFACE

This book was initially prepared from lectures that I did at the Southeast and Southwest Regional Meetings of the American Association of Pastoral Counselors (AAPC) in the fall of 2001. My intent in the lectures was to focus on the conversations contained in the book of Job as a model for developing a cross-cultural perspective on God conversation. Basic questions posed by the book of Job are, Why do innocents suffer? Where is God in the midst of tragedy? How can we discern God's presence in the midst of the carnage, pain, and suffering?

When I delivered the lectures at the Southeast Region of AAPC, long-time friend and colleague Burrell Dinkins helped me see how giving privilege to my own conversation with God enabled me to deal with my struggles with death, pain, and suffering. His question to me was, Does God help us privilege God conversation by asking us questions? He then asked me the question that brought significant insight to my own life and to this book. He asked, "Did not God teach you to privilege God conversation by asking you questions in the same way God asked Job questions?"

My answer to this question was a resounding, "Yes!" I recalled how God came to me in a still small voice during my recovery from quadruple bypass heart surgery. God had asked me if I could accept the healing that God brought to my life. My answer was yes, although I really did not know the full ramifications of that question. The surgery was in December 1994, and since then the meaning of God's question has shaped the way I live my life. For me, the ultimate meaning of God's question had to do with fulfilling my call with boldness and living the kind of holistic life that keeps me alive doing God's will. My heart problems, as it turned out, were related to lifestyle rather than to any family health heritage. The basic lessons for me were to become a vegetarian and to learn to be comfortable with intimacy. God valued my life; the least I could do was bring my view of myself in line with God's.

As the book continued to develop, the precise focus of it began to surface. I was more interested in the theodicy question as it relates to African Americans and our pilgrimage here in the United States. My concern for why the innocent suffer became more specific to African Americans. Thus, the dominant question became, Why has God allowed African Americans to suffer slavery and racism because of our skin color? Two related questions became, How have we as African Americans lived with dignity and honor despite the presence of the evils of slavery and racism? and How have we as African Americans resisted recruitment into negative identities or combated the pressure to become victims of the racial conversations existing in wider society? Thus, the primary focus shifted to the sacred identity formation of African Americans and what we can learn from it generally for all people.

This book attempts to answer two perennial questions: What does it mean to be persons of worth and value in our contemporary culture? and How can a relationship with God give us a renewed sense of our worth and value?

The thesis of this book is that we become persons by internalizing the conversations in which we take part, but we become *holy* persons by giving conversation with God a privileged status over all other conversations. Conversations with God, then, are personal interchanges with God. They transcend human conversations and bring insight into our human condition in profound ways. As a result of these conversations with God, we gain a fuller understanding of our worth and value. While we may not always know the difference between the voice of God and the voices that otherwise fill our head, we can be assured that we can test our discernment within our Christian community. Where two or more are gathered, Christ is present. God gives us the gift of Christian friends and community to help us with this discernment process.

God also gives us the gift of Scripture. Following the African American tradition of drawing on biblical material, I will use the book of Job, but I will also draw on contemporary African American biography and fiction to show how transformation happens when persons learn to put conversations with God in the forefront. In the book of Job, we meet a man named Job who was honored by all who knew him as a righteous person. Yet, this good man suffers staggering losses and is shamed by well-meaning friends who insist that there is something wrong with him. Surely, he has sinned because God is punishing him. Throughout the narrative, Job sorts through different levels of conversations about human value and worth until God's voice breaks through with wind and fury. Although this biblical story gives no answer to the reason for the suffering of the innocent, it does affirm that God is ever willing to have a relationship with us. God is able to be in relationship with us through personal communication, in this case, through conversation. We can always depend on God to be a conversation partner.

This has certainly been the experience of African Americans in our pilgrimage in the United States of America. We have identified with the plight of Job and his suffering. We have had difficulty understanding why we have been singled out for oppression because of our skin color. While we understood the nature of evil, we still cried out in complaint to God about our undeserved predicament. God heard our complaint and cry and offered us fellowship and conversation. This God conversation and fellowship became the source of our sacred identity as worthwhile and valued people and of our ability to resist being recruited into negative identities. Moreover, this fellowship with God became the reservoir for our courage to pursue the vocation of liberation from slavery and racism.

As in the case with Job, God never answered the question of why we have had to suffer slavery and racism because of our skin color. Nonetheless, God did provide the gift of fellowship; and from this gift of fellowship we have discovered our sacred identity as persons made in the image and likeness of God despite what was being said in wider culture. In fellowship with God we also discovered meaning through vocation. God disclosed to us that we were partners with God in redeeming creation from evil. We also learned that we could live victoriously by resisting recruitment into negative identities. In short, we have learned to overcome racism in all of its manifestations, including our internalization of it, by entering into fellowship with God.

The basic lesson I learned is that God is present in my struggles with life and death concerns. I can depend on God to be present in both the suffering and pain of the recovery process and in the transition from life to death. I can trust God because God sees me as a person endowed with value and worth. And God loves me enough to help me see myself as a person worthy of God's valuation.

God's question posed to me during my recovery from surgery has led me to write this book. I realize that God is the ultimate One who bestows life and worth on all of us as human beings. While I was taught this as a child growing up as an African American Christian, this message had grown dim in my hearing. I needed a fresh word from God.

This book, then, is about sacred identity formation. From an African American faith perspective, sacred identity formation from its inception is something that God does partnering with us. It is the way we are led by God to sort through a variety of cultural conversations and internal conversations about our human worth and value until we can prioritize God conversation the way Job did. Our faith community assists in this process of sacred identity formation by offering fellowship and cues to what privileging God conversation is like. Thus, sacred identity formation is a process of internalizing God conversation, and our faith communities play vital roles in this process.

For many of us, it is too easy to listen to what society tells us to be. In our culture we often hear that we need to be successful, become rich, buy this car, live in this house, get married, have this many children. Sometimes the voices of our culture can seem benign, but sometimes they are malignant. Carrying a gun will make you important. Step on your colleague if he or she gets in your way to the top. Trust nobody. Love only yourself. Get what you can for today. But whether benign or malignant, all of these voices carry with them values derived from the marketplace.

In the marketplace you are only as valuable as the goods you possess. The only things of value you have are the things you can sell in the marketplace—your talent, your skills, your information, your looks. Humans are viewed as commodities that can be bought and sold. What you are worth means how much money you can bring in. One doesn't have to think or go far to see that the highest value in our culture is placed on being white, young, attractive, heterosexual, well-educated, articulate, and rich.

Every day our media bombards us with these values. All the entertainment media—print, television, music, movies, theater—reinforces a particular image of what it means to be a person of worth and value. Compare the messages of the media with the messages of Scripture. In the Bible, being a person of worth and value means being embraced by God's love despite our faults and human limitations.

It was in Paul's claim that "While we were yet sinners, Christ died for us" (from Romans 5:6). It is in God's love for us despite our fallen nature that we find our worth and value. In other words, God's love for us transcends our usefulness and success in the marketplace.

We in the African American community know what it means to be a commodity in the marketplace. Our history is full of its tragedy. Our society even today still harbors the consequences of being bought and sold on the block. We should be the first to say that living by the will of the marketplace leads to destruction. But how can we break free when these market values are in the air we breathe? And many of us are so vulnerable.

Often our only sense of personal worth and value comes about by internalizing certain conversations that take place in our culture. In this culture of weakened generational ties and other social institutions, these market values invade us. We are vulnerable to the voices of the market because other voices are drowned out, even those voices that might offer more appealing alternatives. Alternative, nonmarketing values tend to be relational values related to care, nurture, commitment, and loyalty. Marketing values emphasize, on the other hand, monetary investments, profits, public policies related to taxes, and morality shaped by government and the entertainment industries.

My understanding of sacred identity formation grows out of my Weslyan background. Sacred identity reflects Wesley's therapeutic soteriology.[1] That is, God's grace is at work in our lives restoring our spiritual, emotional, and relational health. It is God's grace that provides the capacity to privilege God conversation since God's prevenient grace comes before our ability to privilege. God's restoring grace enables us to respond to what God is doing to restore our fallen nature and to God's gracious presence at work in our lives. Moreover, it is God's justifying grace that makes us right with God through our repentance and belief in Jesus Christ. Thus, sacred identity formation involves our ability to respond to God's gracious transforming presence in our lives restoring us to our original relationship with God, which was disrupted by the Fall. Wesley's prevenient and justifying grace are about the power to heal our brokenness and our separation from God. Thus, restoration of our original relationship with God constitutes the source of our sacred identity. Sacred identity formation is the developing of this sacred identity in our everyday lives, making our lives more meaningful. In addition to this, sacred identity formation, like identity formation, is a lifelong process; and in the Weslyan language of grace this process is called *sanctification*.

11

The goal of sanctification is the recovery of our likeness to and the moral image of God in our lives.

Wesley's view of justification deals with the human propensity to sin. Job's experience of oppression and the African American experience of racism are not about the sinful natures of those suffering from evil. Therefore, Weslyan therapeutic soteriology is used to cover both the human propensity to sin as well as the relationship that God offers all persons whether they commit sin or are the victims of sin.

This book brings a pastoral theology critique to the commodification and commercial marketing of human images of personhood.[2] From a theological point of view, the images of personhood portrayed in the media and in pursuit of commercial success are contrary to the gospel. These images that market humans as commodities lead to many forms of human bondage including addictions to substances, racial profiling, and other in-group/out-group distinctions that drive wedges between people. The history of racism in this country is rooted in the total commodification of human worth. Here again the African American community has something important to say about the distortion of human worth brought about by the wholesale adoption of market values.

As already indicated, my anthropological perspective used in this book is grounded in biblical and Weslyan theology and rooted in my own experience growing up in a Christian home. Over and over again, I was taught both in my home and in my church that all of us are persons of worth and value in the eyes of God. As an African American sometimes it was hard to hear that affirmation. Often the voices of culture drowned out the voice of God. So often the voices of culture offered only negative and condescending words about who I was as a person. In my church and family the conversation was different. They said I was a gift of God and that I was a person of special promise and worth. But who was I to believe? How did I see myself? Over the years I have increasingly realized that the gift of personhood comes from God. This gift transcends race, gender, creed, national origin, ethnic background, and sexual orientation. This gift of personhood comes directly from God; and even when the voices of the market try to prevail, God will come sometimes with wind and fury, sometimes with a still small voice.

Sometimes people need help. They need help hearing the voice of God or distinguishing its pitch and tenor. Sometimes people are just too wounded to hear anything other than their own suffering and shame. They need a person of God from the faith community to facilitate the process of learning to listen. Persons trained in pastoral counseling and in pastoral theology can help people learn to begin conversations with God and later learn how and what it means to privilege that conversation.

The book of Job illustrates what I mean by giving conversation with God a special, privileged place in one's life. Even in the midst of pain and suffering, God's voice can be heard and conversation with God is possible, even necessary. Contemporary African American biography and fiction provide pastoral counseling and pastoral theology models for helping persons sort through the many voices they hear and the conversations in which they participate. An assumption of this book is that giving conversation with God priority in one's life will transform not only the individual but also the broader community. The possibility of transformation brings hope of redemption to the marketplace and to the destructive values it promotes.

Psychologically, my thoughts are grounded in the concept of internalization promoted in the work of Michael White. For him identity involves taking into the self social conversations in our formative environment. He also focuses on the power that society has in recruiting others into negative identities. His works help to affirm what many African Americans have done since the inception of the Civil Rights movement and prior to it. His works help us to work through those negative images of ourselves that we have internalized from wider society. A more formal presentation of his ideas will come in chapter 6.

The critical point is that the psychological foundation of this book is relational and interactive rather than Freudian and psychoanalytic. The concept of internalization grows out of the psychoanalytic orientation of object relations theory, however. Yet, I employ it based on White's understanding of human discourse and conversation that comes as the result of the development of advanced language and cognitive skills of children. Thus, the use of internalization is more verbal and conversational than the pre-verbal relational emphasis of object relations theory.

From an African American perspective, the emphasis in the book is on how we have appropriated Scripture and theology to understand that we have been affirmed by God despite our being recruited into negative self-images because of racism and oppression. Yes, we were exposed to Christianity and its meaning from those who enslaved us, but we creatively appropriated what we heard and were taught to meet our own needs for liberation and freedom. We refashioned the meaning we learned in ways that gave us agency and full participation in making our own meaning. The way we appropriated the Scripture and theology gave us a sense of participation and power in the creation of the meaning for our own lives. Those who believe that we were contaminated or cloned into a slave mentality by Christianity misunderstand the nature of how oppressed people have used their cultural heritage and exposure to faith to fashion a unique approach to life.

I have mentioned John Wesley and Michael White as critical sources as I developed this book along with an interpretation of the book of Job. The appropriation of what is important from these sources reflects an indigenous method of constructing meaning based on the cultural and faith experiences we brought with us from Africa to interpret our experiences here in the diaspora. Thus, my use of these authors reflects the peculiar interpretation that is consistent with our African American experience. At some point it may differ from what non–African Americans have gleaned from these same sources. This is how the creative method of cultural appropriation functions.

This book is not just for African Americans. It is not about how one ethnic minority group comes to grips with negative cultural images. It is about *all* of us—talking to God, letting God shape and transform us and our world. It is about making God a conversation partner in the midst of our diversity so that we all can experience the sacred worth of each other.

Finally, my sister-in-law, Margaret Wimberly, and the Abingdon Press staff did a wonderful job proofing and copyediting this book. It is possible to write with confidence when you know there are others who will read the work to assure its communicability.

Notes

1. Randy L. Maddox, *Responsible Grace: John Wesley's Practical Theology* (Nashville: Kingswood Books, 1994), 83.
2. Sylvia Anne Hewlett and Cornel West, *War Against Parents* (New York: Houghton Mifflin, 1998), 20-29.

THE QUEST FOR WORTH AND VALUE

What does it mean to be persons of worth and value in our contemporary culture? Whatever the answers, the fact that we perennially raise questions such as this suggest that we humans are always interested in constructing meaning. But meaning comes into being through the mediation of particular communities. That is to say, through our living together, through socially constructed categories, we each, both individually and communally, construct our definition of what it means to be worthy and valued.

My thesis is that the meaning-building process comes about through conversations between individuals, between individuals and groups, and between groups. I am using the term *conversation* in the broadest possible sense—as interpersonal communication. Through this communication, persons come to understand in some limited way what it means to be *me* in this particular place and time. I hope I also learn what it means for *you* to be you here as well; further, we need to learn what it means to be *us* here and now.

Being in conversation also means that there can be a number of conversation partners. These partners are not necessarily equal, but the word *conversation* always means that all persons involved have an active part, no matter how small. This does not mean, however, that all parties have to talk in order to be in conversation. Some of the *least* productive conversations I have ever had have been when everybody was talking. But one has to be *engaged* to be in conversation, even if one only listens. Likewise, some of my best conversations have been when I simply listened to what others said.

Engagement in conversation does not mean that there is understanding, but it does mean that I am trying to find meaning in what you say. For example, a young child may not truly understand that he or she needs a nap, let alone why; but the child can determine from your tone of voice and gestures that you seriously mean what you say. Even infants engage with others by gazing with their eyes, and they disengage by averting their gaze.

But of course, not all conversations are equal. Some conversations carry more weight than others; some conversation participants are more important than others. Some conversations are more believable; some carry more social reinforcement. From bits and pieces of those conversations that grab our attention, we organize our life. Some of these organizing conversations gradually take priority and become central to our life story. Some conversations that we hear come from our faith communities and can give us clues as to what values are significant for shaping our lives in the world. As we participate in the worship and educational life of the faith community, we slowly begin to organize our lives around these conversations; and certain faith stories began to orient us to the meaning and purposes for our lives. Such participation in faith communities leads us toward high-priority conversations that have a privileged place within our inner being. In fact, we are all searching for those conversations and stories that offer us maximum meaning in our lives. We seek to avoid, if at all possible, those conversations and stories that don't offer meaningful purposes and helpful opportunities for fulfilling our lives. We need those positive conversations and stories to help us build a sense of self and other.

As we internalize and prioritize conversations, some conversations become the standard by which new conversations are measured and evaluated. Through this interpersonal process we come to understand our world and our place in it. We also come to understand who we are and our place as a group in relation to my place as an individual. For example, I remember conversations with my father about the nature of intelligence. I used to believe that good grades in school were a matter of having the gift of intelligence and that good grades would come easy for those who had that gift. Therefore, I believed that studying was wasted effort since I believed I did not have the gift of intelligence. As a young child, I had internalized societal beliefs about my intelligence as a black child. My father would counter this by entering into conversation and telling me about his college roommate who always made good grades. His roommate would party and brag about how he did not need to study. No one other than my father ever saw him studying. My father said that his roommate would wait until everyone went to bed, and then he would study all night. My father's point was to provide me with an alternative conversation and story that would challenge my internalized belief in my own inferiority.

Societal conversations are very powerful and have shaping properties for our lives. Many of our wider cultural conversations are helpful and should be internalized. However, other conversations, particularly those wrapped up in class and negative racial valuation, need to be countered with other conversations coming from our primary relational communities early in our development.

Every conversation carries with it a valuation of who I am in relation to you and who you are in relation to me, including how I feel and think about you. Conversations can also never be completely separated from the power dynamics that transpire between people. From these often competing valuations, persons develop their deepest convictions and beliefs about life and what it means to live in their world.[1] For example, some conversations are self-esteem building and others are not. If we encounter negative conversations over and over again, they tend to have a pejorative impact on how we feel about ourselves. Negative conversations produce negative evaluations of ourselves. The experience of continually being in positive conversations with others will facilitate and build positive self-esteem within us. Positive conversations enable us to evaluate ourselves in positive ways. Our social involvement and discourse with others provide us with opportunities to take into ourselves either bad or good sources of self-evaluation, particularly in the early phases of our lives.

To some extent, every conversation is an encapsulation of an entire relationship. Said differently, every conversation is an episode in the entire web of relationships. That is to say that every dynamic present in a particular relationship, including the past and anticipated future, is present in some way; and every conversation depends to some degree on all previous conversations with the particular parties and how conversations typically go: "I always win," or "You always come off getting the best of me." The point is that human discourse and conversation provide for us the rules for how we should relate with others and the world. From all of the interactions we are able to discern specific rules of interaction that tell us what is significant, important, and valuable about ourselves and others.

From the point of view of faith narratives, we learn to privilege certain values and ideas over others. Faith narratives provide a hierarchy of values that help us select between competing values and conflicting stories. For example, many faith stories in the Judeo-Christian tradition are about agape love or neighbor love. There are also secular stories that promote self-interest love in ways that exclude neighbor love. These are two competing conversations, but our faith narratives help us prioritize the selfless form of love.

The Importance of Conversation for Pastoral Theology

The concept of conversation is important for pastoral theology. As mentioned earlier, conversation is *interpersonal* communication. Thus, for Christians, conversation with God is possible. Many theologians would say that not only is conversation with God possible, but for us to be fully human, conversation with God is necessary. And for us to have the truest sense of our worth and value, we need to look to the living God as revealed in Scripture.

From my African American Christian upbringing, I was taught to privilege conversations with God as the ultimate granter and guarantor of human worth and value. I was taught by my parents and my church community that God had a purpose for my life, and that life consisted of finding out what that purpose was. My task was to carry it out. Discovering God's purpose for my life, I was taught, came from encountering God in my everyday walk with God and in conversations with God. I was encouraged to enter into conversation with God through prayer. I was taught consistently and well, but many are not as fortunate. As pastoral theologians, we must minister to all types of persons, including those who are too wounded or who lack the energy to engage in much conversation.

Two books from my publishing career help spell out the influence of my own religious heritage. These books are *Liberation and Human Wholeness: The Conversion Experiences of Black People in Slavery and Freedom* and *Recalling Our Own Stories: Spiritual Renewal for Religious Caregivers.*[2] Both books give credence to the centrality of God conversation as a central heritage of African American Christianity.

In this chapter, I want to begin the exploration of privileging conversation with God with a case illustration. Second, I want to correlate therapeutic conversation with the theological insights that emerge from the case. Third, I will draw on the book of Job as a model of privileging God conversation as a way to discuss its transformative power in order to confirm universal human worth and dignity.

Case Illustration

In his autobiography, *Death Dance: A True Story of Drug Addiction and Redemption,*[3] Clifford Harris recounts his miraculous transformation from a chronic substance abuser to a drug-free advocate for the role of faith in recovery. His story represents a pattern I want to emphasize, because it approaches the way I want to talk about privileging conversation with God. This pattern mirrors what I see in Scripture as well as in some contemporary novels by African Americans.

In his book, Clifford unfolds his journey toward putting God first in his life. For Clifford this means conversing with God in such a way that he comes to have a deepened understanding of his personal worth and value. He learns to give conversation with God top priority in his life and to listen to God's voice to the exclusion of all other voices.

As we read Clifford's story, we see his transformation slowly taking place. Initially we see Clifford marred in the problem-saturated and deficit-laden conversations of his early life. He was recruited into stories early in his life that led him into a prolonged period of substance abuse and stealing to support his addiction. He finally came to a place where more self-authenticating stories and conversations began to take center stage at midlife. The setting for this new self-authenticating conversation was a prison where transformation took place within a cell and a library.

As Harris learns to give priority to his conversations with God, he also comes to see himself as a child of God, endowed with a sacred value and worth. Through conversation with God, Clifford begins to see himself from God's point of view. He sees what God wants him to become, and he sees the kinds of relationships God wants him to have. As these holy conversations become a part of who Clifford Harris is, they become part of his sacred identity. He finds himself embraced by God's unmerited grace that affirms his value and worth despite what he had done in his life to himself and others. He also discovers what God is calling him to become and what he is supposed to be doing with his life.

Many theologians, especially in the Wesleyan Protestant tradition, talk about this process as *sanctification*, the process whereby God leads us through grace into a life of holiness. Some theologians talk about this process as reclaiming the *imago dei* within the self. Still others talk about this as growing into the image of Christ. The process of sanctification begins with a renewed relationship with God through the power of grace. From this relationship the image of God is restored in us, and we begin to take on the character of God as well as Godlikeness. The perfection of love becomes an ongoing process as we begin to fulfill God's calling on our lives.

From a very early age, Clifford thought he was different. Many people have these same feelings, but for Clifford they became crippling. Clifford's earliest inner conversations reinforced his feelings of being different from his family. He describes himself standing in front of the mirror comparing himself to his brothers and sisters. He would touch his skin and feel his hair. Although his skin was dark like his father's, he often wondered if he was adopted. He just did not look like his other brothers and sisters. His feelings of being different intensified when members of his family referred to him as the "ugly boy." He felt that his entire family conspired to label him as not only different but repulsive. Although Clifford says his family may have meant it as a joke, it was no joke. These words wounded him and became a poisoning conversation that came to characterize how he thought about himself. This conversation became a defining characteristic of his identity of worthlessness.

Although Clifford did not realize it, his concept of ugly had wider sources in the culture. He learned early, as do most of us, that society prefers light skin and straight hair. Those ethnic groups that have these characteristics are valued more highly than those that do not. Of course, some members of his own family had these same physical qualities, but he did not. As a result, his family became mediators of the message that not only was he different but he was worth less as a human being because he lacked certain physical characteristics.

Not all of Clifford's conversations from his childhood were negative, however. His parents were devout Seventh-Day Adventists, and their faith played a big part in their life. His parents taught him and his siblings to be loving, honest, and respectful of God and others. There were also strict rules governing traditional personal piety. This piety was in the form of daily family prayer and devotion. They also had family worship at the beginning of each day. There was a lot of family singing with words that later would become the language of his conversations with God. He enjoyed going to church interacting with family friends. At some deep level, Clifford internalized conversations that he was truly a child of God with worth and value. But these conversations were silenced as he encountered conversations in a society that devalued him because of his race.

All families, no matter how religious, have difficulties. As mentioned earlier, Clifford felt branded by his family as an outsider. These negative feelings were further reinforced by the rejection he felt by the family member with whom he most closely identified—his father. Clifford's father worked very hard, but from Clifford's point of view his father seemed to prefer his work to being with his son. Even though Clifford worked as an apprentice under his father, Clifford never felt that he belonged. He always felt like he was on the outside looking in.

In addition, Clifford's father was a brick mason, a job that required moving the family frequently. As a young man, Clifford may have realized that his father was doing the best he could, but he could not forgive his father for not being able to give him what he needed—a valued place with people who loved him. In pastoral counseling one often sees adults vent hurt and anger toward parents who were simply incapable of being the kind of person their child needed. Most of us have imperfect parents, and we all have to offer forgiveness at least within our own souls to our parents for failing us.

Moving from one school to another following his father's job brought Clifford in direct contact with the white world. When they moved to Colorado, there were no segregated schools, and Clifford was often the only black person in his class. Even though there was no segregation, Clifford still felt racial attitudes and stereotypes shaped his teachers' attitudes toward him. Again and again, he felt singled out for his teacher's abuse. Again and again, he got the message that he did not belong. So he rebelled. His attitude became, "You don't want me to belong, so I won't." Unfortunately, his rebellion only served to force him out of school altogether.

By twelve years of age, Clifford had lost his childhood. No longer being a child meant that he had to go to work. Not only had he internalized conversations that he did not belong; he now believed that his feelings did not count at all. Clifford worked with his father who worked Clifford as hard as any full-grown man. It must have looked to Clifford that he had the responsibilities of being a man, but none of the benefits; so Clifford decided to *take* the benefits he could by rebelling in a big way: becoming involved in drug abuse, stealing, and gambling. At least he could be something in a big way. Perhaps not as a willing participate at first, but slowly many of Clifford's conversations brought him only the pain of bondage and self-destruction. Now, Clifford did not even have a place in law-abiding society. In a literal sense, he was an outlaw.

At the age of forty-four and in prison, Clifford began to hear the voice of a distant conversation. He was at a point in his life where he was ready to transcend the problem-saturated and crisis-laden conversations characterizing his past. He was ready to begin an inner conversation that would reexamine these negative stories in his life and initiate a re-editing process that eventually led him to transformation. As this conversation began to come to the fore, it brought with it a sense of liberation.

While in prison, he came to the sudden awareness that God must be keeping him alive for something special. It suddenly occurred to him that others who did the same exact things he was doing were dead. Why not him? He had reused contaminated syringes in the shooting galleries, but never contracted HIV; his dancing with death remained flirting. He was trying to do his death dance, but someone kept cutting in. Someone was interfering with his death dance, and Clifford began to believe there was a reason he was still alive. As these liberating, affirming conversations began to stake their claim, Clifford came to realize that he was only alive because God wanted him alive for some mysterious reason.

The fact that his life had been spared time after time became a topic of his inner conversation. As he puzzled over this, he would go to the prison library. Initially he went just because there was a female librarian, and he found it helpful to his soul to be in her presence. She unknowingly offered a respite to his inner turmoil. In order to hide the true reason he went to the library, Clifford browsed the shelves pretending to be interested in reading. Then one day he spotted a book. It was a copy of the same book his parents had read at those family prayer occasions years ago. The very sight of that book made Clifford realize that his inner turmoil was spiritual in nature, and he sensed that the stirring within himself was refreshing.

The book was about the life of Jesus. Warm memories of love and acceptance began to return to his consciousness. As affirming conversations took shape over the course of many months, the old self-sabotaging conversations receded like the ebbing tide. He felt as though he was in the grip of an inner transformation that would not let him go. At first he just checked the book out, leaving it unopened. He needed only to look at the book as a reminder; he already knew the content. The book eventually brought him to the place where he could begin, once again, to have direct conversation with God. A missing piece of his life fell into place; and as it found its rightful place, he began to find his.

No longer an outsider, conversation with God gave Clifford an abiding sense of belonging. Now all other conversations had to be interpreted by this new, liberating conversation. His transformation healed him when he was able to maintain the privileged position he had given conversation with God, letting this conversation push the old, binding ones away. His transformation became healing for others when he began to tell his story letting others see the benefits of being God's beloved child.

Pastoral Theological Reflection

The question is: *How can pastoral counseling help people learn to privilege God conversation?* To answer this, pastoral theology draws upon the wealth of human experience, including behavioral science. Using behavioral science can help us understand the transformation process that enables persons to prioritize their relationship with God. Specifically, I will look at membership theory and externalization theory.

Membership Theory

While there was a rich resource of religious and spiritual imagery that could help facilitate Clifford's inner conversations connecting him to God, there were also disconnecting images and disjointed conversations. These disjointed conversations not only drowned out the voice of God with a cacophony of noise, they distorted other potential healing voices.

One loving voice that Clifford yearned to hear was that of his father, but instead he heard only rejection. Instead of hearing voices of friends inviting him to join in healthy camaraderie, Clifford heard the voices of his childhood peers and teachers telling him what an outsider he was.

Perhaps the most devastating conversation was in the wider social arena. Because society largely dismisses African American culture, most vividly symbolized by its devaluing of black skin, Clifford had nowhere to go. That is to say that Clifford already felt like an outsider rejected by his own family, especially his father. As his world grew beyond the confines of his family, he found rejection at school. He did finally find acceptance among peers, but being an insider with them only served to place him outside the law. Clifford felt he had nowhere to go to be valued and held in esteem until he heard the voice of God stirring in his memory.

Despite the noise it created, Clifford was engaged in the conversation of the wider society. We all take part in this mega-conversation. Just as we breathe in the air around us, we imbibe the conversations of our various cultures within the broader society. With so many ongoing conversations, one has to ask, How does a person choose between them? How does one choose to listen to some conversations over others? Why did Clifford engage destructive conversations that silenced the rich faith conversations of his family and with God?

As mentioned earlier in this book, conversations are not value neutral. They carry with them socially constructed meanings and values. Here I want to say that neither are conversations impartial in that conversations have a way of recruiting conversation partners.

Recruiting is a process of drawing people into conversations that build the larger stories of society. Recruiting as such is not a sinister process, but it does tend to support and reinforce the plot of the overall narrative. This means that there are always vested interests in continuing the story and the conversations that make up the story. Every story embodies particular values and evaluations. For example, in pastoral counseling we try to get counselees to review the stories that have made dominant claims on their lives. Such claims help form the person's predominant feelings about himself or herself. Such claims may be negative or positive depending on the kind of review counselees make. The role of the pastoral counselor is to help people review these story claims and the impact that they have had. Counselors also help counselees re-edit or re-author these stories if they prove to have negative impact on personal growth.

Because people are recruited into *particular* conversations,[4] they don't know *all* of the repercussions of their engagement. How could they? Social narratives are always much bigger than particular persons or even groups of persons. These narratives are also the context for our particular conversations. As the context, social narratives circumscribe the possibilities from which we choose; they set the limits, define our universe. This is not to say, however, that we are trapped inside our particular context, because as Christians, we believe that God is the author of the overarching narrative. We may be limited, but we are not trapped because God offers us freedom to transcend particular conversations and to be transformed and equipped to fully live.

Becoming liberated from negative and limiting conversations is a long process. This process involves reviewing the conversations that have shaped one's life, including identifying them, assessing how they have impacted our lives, and deciding to privilege other or different conversations that are more growth facilitating. Although stories shape who we are, we can transform these stories and participate in shaping the stories that impact our lives.

Clifford was recruited into conversations that disconnected him from meaningful conversations with his family and significant others. He was isolated from other people that could boost his sense of true worth. Because his developing sense of worth had been so defaced, certainly by the age of twelve—although it was crippled much earlier—the sense of self he had was also devalued, making him a prime candidate for further recruitment.

The process of separating persons from their original meaning legacies and recruiting them into alienating conversations and stories is called *dismembership*.[5] The goal of this process is to separate persons from their original meaningful memberships, the end result being loss of meaning and purpose.[6] Clifford's problems with substance abuse came as the result of dis-membership from his original meaning context and recruitment into an alien conversation. To be sure, Clifford and his family contributed to these two processes, but conversation in the wider society about skin color further affected Clifford in a negative way. Although, there were competing conversations to counter the effects of these processes, Clifford could not resist. While it would be interesting to know more about Clifford in order to have a better understanding of why he could not resist, whatever the ultimate reason, Clifford is like countless others: He was tempted beyond his endurance.

Dis-membership is a dominant conversation in a culture where human worth is commodified in the marketplace. Membership suggests commitment to relationships, caring, and nurturing.[7] These values run counter to today's marketing values. Being uprooted, as Clifford was, from the security of a local community so his father could pursue work and constantly changing schools contributed to Clifford's sense of belonging to no place, being disconnected, and feeling alienated. While families can survive economically by being constantly uprooted, the consequences of being alienated are hard for children to overcome. Children can literally feel dismembered. It took Clifford until his midforties before he could recover, and that recovery took a miracle.

Externalization

We grow, develop, and interpret life through internalizing conversations that take place across generations and within a variety of contexts—home, school, work, church, and play.[8] From Clifford, we learn that there are families-of-origin conversations that result from our membership in families. There are also cohort conversations or same-generation conversations with peers. There are also faith conversations that take place within the church that are multigenerational. All these conversations impact us, but it is our responsibility to take them into ourselves and to make decisions about how they influence our lives. Yes, interaction and experience within different groups and conversations affect us, but we still have agency or the ability to create meaning through the process of privileging.

The point of pastoral counseling is to make sure that we increase our agency or our ability to privilege. Privileging is a process of articulating our current story and the conversations that go into making up our stories, assessing the story and its impact on our current life, and deciding to re-author or re-edit the story conversations.

Essentially, pastoral counseling provides the space for examining the negative conversations that we have internalized, but counseling is also about facilitating the privileging of positive conversations so that one can move forward in one's life and vocation. Clifford internalized two major conversations in his life; one was positive and the other was negative. The negative conversation was one that led him into life circumstances that demeaned his self-esteem and curtailed his growth. The positive conversation built his self-esteem and enhanced his capacity for growth into the image of God.

Human striving for meaning is never fully satisfied with negative conversations. Negative stories always impoverish the person; positive stories enhance and enrich. Negative stories lead us away from God and ultimately to sin and death; positive stories lead us toward a relationship with God. There is something within us that lures us to internalize positive stories and conversations that give our lives true meaning and purpose. Thus, we are never satisfied with negative conversations, although we might settle for them—for a while. In all of our lives the positive conversations will always be working to surface to our awareness despite other negative conversations at work in us. Although defaced or distorted, the image of God lives within each of us. It is dynamic and thus pushes to realize itself despite the negative conversations and stories that we internalize.

Sometimes we have competing positive images taking place in our lives, but we cannot actualize one without denying the other. In such cases, it is important to make the best choice given all the circumstances and options. It is important, however, to make choices that are consistent with the best options that we have realizing that life as lived is an unfolding plot. Even bad choices don't have to be disastrous when we realize that plots thicken and twist several times before God's purposes for our growth and development are fulfilled. When we make choices, we must make them in faith realizing that God can be part of our maturation process.

Clifford's original God conversation was never completely obliterated by other conversations. It was silenced but never eliminated. Slowly, the inner drive for positive meaning reemerged and the childhood conversation with God unfolded in growing force and power when Clifford was in prison. The book about Jesus became the central focus of his life, and its very presence evoked warm memories that reconnected him at first with his memory of his earlier conversation with God and then with direct conversation with God. Reconnecting with former memberships is called re-membership.[9]

Indeed, re-membership took place in Clifford's life, but it set off another process within Clifford. This process is called *externalization*.[10] The other side of internalizing conversations is externalizing them. Such a process is not the same as psychological projection, which defends the ego from anxiety. Rather, this process is the ego looking directly at the conversation basis of one's personality. It assumes psychological or ego strength and a desire to grow. It comes when a person realizes that his or her life, up to that point, has been lived trying to avoid internal pain. Externalization is the decision to face the pain caused by privileging negative stories and conversations.

Externalization refers to the process of reflection that helps persons look at ways their recruitment takes place and the impact that recruitment has on growth and development.[11] A point of externalization is to lessen the impact of negative conversations and to promote more positive conversations through exploring one's recruitment. Clifford's process of externalizing negative conversations involved writing his autobiography. Writing gave him a way to review his life and map the ways he was influenced by particular conversations. Thus, his book *Death Dance* is the completion of a process of externalization. This process allowed him to explore negative conversations and to reflect on his conversations with God.

Negative conversations with others affect our conversations with God. There is a long-standing psychological principle that our relationships with others color our relationship with God. This is very true until we are put in a situation where we experience God apart from our past relationships. Our past dictates our relationship with God until we have a chance to encounter God beyond those relationships. Job helps us to understand this process.

Insights from the Book of Job

The book of Job is a series of conversations. It opens with a conversation between God and Satan, and much of the book contains conversations between Job and his friends. The climax of the book is, of course, God's conversation with Job; and the book concludes with a short narrative section.

At the beginning of the book, Job is a man highly honored and esteemed by his community. He has all the qualities of being a good religious man; he has been blessed with plenty. Job's efforts have been fruitful and God has multiplied his wealth. There is also the implication that it is because God has blessed Job that Job is esteemed by his community. There is an element of surprise, then, when catastrophe strikes Job. "God would only punish Job if he had sinned," his neighbors thought.

Of course, we the readers are in the unusual position of knowing that God and Satan have a wager. So we know that Job's sufferings are not his fault. The question is not, Whose fault is Job's situation? Although, many of us do wonder. The question the Scripture seems to ask is, What is Job going to do about it? How is he going to respond? Not, what *can* he do? Cursing God and dying is not an option for Job. Rather, by asking what Job is going to do in this untenable situation, and how he will bear the full force of shame, the writer focuses our attention on Job.

Obviously the book of Job says something about God, that God is always present even in our suffering. But the book says more about the person, Job. In the book we see Job's faithfulness and steadfastness to God even when God's faithfulness and steadfastness to Job are not so clear. In fact if one understands Job's twofold restoration at the end of the book as God's compensation for injustice done, Job appears vindicated. Does God have to regain our respect by the end of the book?

Job's community, represented by his friends, also has a vested interest in his honor. The more honorable a person was, the more he gave and was expected to give to the community. His friends' insistence that Job must have sinned was because they knew they hadn't. They weren't responsible for his losses and shame. Johs Pedersen says that if the blessing of wealth, children, crops, and cattle departed so that he could no long give to the community, so did honor, according to the wisdom of ancient Israel.

To be valued in Job's society meant being honorable and successful in all that one did.[12] In the book of Job, we see Job going from being a highly honored man to what one might call "the least of these." His honor quickly plummets to shame as his losses increase.[13] Pedersen says:

> Job himself has described it to us in bitter words. The harmony has crumbled to pieces; his friends are not to be found; those nearest to him, his wife and children hate him. His slave does not answer him; boys who formerly concealed themselves from his strength, show him contempt (Job 19:13-19); rabble which he would have disdained to have set with the dogs of his flock, deride him (30:1).[14]

Finally, suffering from poverty and physical and emotional pain, Job enters into the series of conversations. Through these first conversations with his friends, Job externalizes the prevailing conversations that are part and parcel of his culture. The wisdom of the time equated wealth and prosperity with favor from God. Likewise, it equated poverty and suffering with God's punishment. The scenario as played out meant wealth became righteousness and honor; poverty became sinfulness and shame. The logic dictated that the converse was also true: righteousness and honor were wealth, and sinfulness and shame were poverty. Into this prevailing narrative comes the episode of Job. Here is a righteous and honorable person who is poor and stricken. Here is an impoverished wretch who is not being punished; he is innocent. He is poor but worthy, suffering yet valued by God. How could this be?

No doubt Job had internalized the ancient teachings, but they made no sense in his current situation. As Job converses with his friends, one could say that he uses his conversation with them as a means to externalize the impact of the cultural conversation represented by the ancient teachings. Through his friends Job (and the reader) sorts through the thorny issues. This sorting becomes a means by which Job gradually comes into conversation with God. One way to view the book of Job is as Job learning to privilege conversation with God in order to move beyond the conventional wisdom.[15]

There are six levels of conversation in which Job engages. First, Job recognizes that the prevailing ancient wisdom was inadequate to speak to his present situation of suffering and loss (9:1-35). Second, he begins to denounce the ancient wisdom as part of the dominant conversation. Third, he begins to consider alternative conversations rooted in his belief that even though it appears that God has abandoned him, Job still trusts God.

> "For I know that my Redeemer lives,
>   and that at the last he will stand upon the earth;
> and after my skin has been thus destroyed,
>   then in my flesh I shall see God." (19:25-26)

Fourth, this declaration of faith marks a transition period when a new conversation within Job begins to emerge and take initiative. Fifth, the new conversation gives way to direct conversation with God (38:1–42:6) such that Job feels vindicated. Finally, sixth, Job gives his conversation a privileged position above all other conversations.

From the book of Job, we can glean a model by which persons can come to a fuller understanding of their worth and value. This model is a process of discovery through conversation first with others and finally with God. As pastoral counselors we often take the role of one of the friends (although, we hope counselors are more insightful), helping the person externalize various cultural conversations clearing the way for a fresh encounter with God.

While it is true many persons face obstacles and challenges to engaging God in conversation, both the cases of Clifford Harris and Job suggest that despite circumstances and woundedness, all that is needed to engage with God is the willingness to do so. God is always willing to engage us. And God is always present wooing us through grace to engage God.

Summary

In our current society the dominant values reflect our marketing culture. We are all recruited into conversations that suggest that some persons are worth more than others. African Americans are also recruited into negative identities as well because of their skin color. Yet, we have an opportunity to transcend these destructive conversations through engaging God as a conversation partner. Through our relationship with God we can see ourselves and others as sacred children of God with identities that stem from God's point of view rather than culture's.

Like Clifford Harris and Job, we are wounded. Many of us have been dismembered, devalued, shamed, or commodified. But like both Clifford and Job there is a possibility that we can be transformed through conversation with God if we simply will.

Notes

1. How we evaluate ourselves based on conversations is found in Edward P. Wimberly, *Moving From Shame to Self-Worth: Preaching and Pastoral Care* (Nashville: Abingdon Press, 1999).

2. Edward P. Wimberly and Anne Streaty Wimberly, *The Conversion Experiences of Black People in Slavery and Freedom* (Nashville: Abingdon Press, 1986) and *Recalling Our Own Stories: Spiritual Renewal for Religious Caregivers* (San Francisco: Jossey-Bass, 1997).

3. Clifford Harris, *Death Dance: A True Story of Drug Addiction and Redemption* (Grand Terrance, Calif.: Drug Alternative Program, 1999).

4. Michael White, *Re-authoring Lives: Interviews and Essays* (Adelaide, South Australia: Dulwich Centre Publications, 1995), 48.

5. Michael White, *The Narratives of Therapist's Lives* (Adelaide, South Australia: Dulwich Centre Publications, 1997), 11.

6. Ibid., 17.

7. Sylvia Ann Hewlett and Cornel West, *War Against Parents* (New York: Houghton Mifflin, 1998), 29-30.

8. Michael White, *Reflections on Narrative Practice: Essays and Interviews* (Adelaide: South Australia: Dulwich Centre Publications, 2000), 3-7.

9. White, *The Narratives of Therapist's Lives*, 23.

10. White, *Reflections on Narrative Practice*, 3.

11. White, *Re-authoring Lives*, 41-59.

12. The insights about honor and shame in ancient Israel come from Johs Pedersen, *Israel: Its Life and Culture* (London: Oxford University Press, 1964), 213-16.

13. Ibid., 215.

14. Ibid., 215-16.

15. Insight into the role of conversation in the book of Job can be gleaned from J. Gerald Janzen, *Job, Interpretation: A Bible Commentary for Teaching and Preaching* (Atlanta: John Knox, 1985), 56-60.

CHAPTER TWO

I AM MORE THAN AN ANIMAL

Pastoral Theology and Sacred Identity Formation

In the previous chapter Clifford Harris began the transformation process when he remembered nurturing conversations from his childhood. These recollections were religious and spiritual in nature. As these memories came forth, the process of giving them privilege over other memories began. As a result, conversations with God also emerged, and these led Clifford to speak directly with God. In short, faith in God was a part of Clifford's identity. But as Clifford began to give conversation with God a prominent place, his identity also began to change. No longer was Clifford the "ugly boy"; he was in truth a beloved son of God. Through conversation with God, Clifford began to see his sacred value and worth from God's point of view; therefore, he began to nurture a sense of sacred worth.

The hallmark of one's sense of the sacred is that once one begins to claim it as part of one's own identity, one then begins to look for the sacred in other people. Seeking and then nurturing the sacred identity in others means that one sees others as cherished children of God. An inevitable consequence of Clifford's transformation was that the more he understood himself as a child of God, the more he was able to see others as his brothers and sisters in God irrespective of their physical characteristics.

The critical question for this chapter is, How do persons begin the process of privileging conversation with God when they do not have a faith tradition to draw upon? Clifford Harris had warm childhood memories of God and church, but many others have memories of a less positive sort or none at all. Clifford's faith was *reawakened*; how do people with no or little background in a faith tradition begin their spiritual *awakening*?

In his book *A Lesson Before Dying*,[1] Ernest J. Gaines tells the story of Jefferson, a man shaped by street conversations. In this masterfully written drama, Gaines describes Jefferson's transformation from one who survives purely on animal instinct to a fully functioning human being with a significant purpose to fulfill before he dies. Jefferson, when we first meet him, survives as a scavenger, preying on the small and weak. He is a predator driven to satisfy basic, untamed animal instincts. If it can be said that he lives by a philosophy, he lives by "survival of the slickest." "Immediate satisfaction" is his motto.

When the story opens, Jefferson's primary conversation is between the legal authorities and his basic instincts. The legal authorities are his conscience, and they present condemning voices. There is no God conversation, and neither is there any evidence that there had ever been any God conversation. There appears to be no evidence of anything religious to draw on in his life, even if he wanted to. He appears to be incapable of being anything other than selfish. He has no idea of how to distinguish right from wrong. All he knows is that legal authorities have told him that he invariably chooses the wrong. By all appearances Jefferson is not a likely candidate for spiritual transformation. He is ignorant of God and all of God's ways. Yet, Gaines gives the reader a glimmer of hope, because if conversation with God is possible for Jefferson, it is possible for anyone.

The goal of this chapter is to use Gaines's book to explore how a person without the benefit of previous religious conversation can come into a relationship with God. Moreover, the chapter can help us see how external voices of condemnation can be silenced by new affirming conversations when one becomes a vital part of a caring community. The point is that we are not condemned to live as victims of the bigger or stronger. While negative conversations may affect us, we do not have to succumb to them. Indeed, conversation with God has transforming power even if one does not have a vital faith heritage. In other words, we are not condemned by our childhoods. Living and growing in God's grace is possible for everyone.

As pastoral theologians, we are not obliged to accept the wisdom that comes to us from secular literature. Our task is to evaluate all wisdom using criteria from our own faith tradition and from our experience as pastoral counselors. Thus, in this chapter, I will evaluate Gaines's understanding of spiritual transformation using my own theological anthropology. In the next section, I will briefly explore the pastoral theological method used in this chapter and throughout this book.

Pastoral Theology

Many pastoral theologians use what is called the revised correlational method. This methodology has its roots in the correlational method that was developed by Paul Tillich. In the correlational method, philosophical or psychological analysis of existence raises certain questions. These questions then shape the form of the theological responses or answers. The importance of this method is that it allowed Tillich to incorporate psychological and other social scientific understanding and vocabulary into his theology. Tillich's aim then was to help theology and theological symbols make sense in their given cultural context.

The problem with Tillich's methodology was that it implied a one-way conversation between theology and social science with social science doing all the asking and theology doing all the responding. Other theologians, such as David Tracy, began to point out that conversation between theology and social science should be more mutual. That is, both theology and social science raising questions and giving answers; both shaping and being shaped by the other. This newer methodology became known as the revised correlational method. This methodology has been used by Don Browning, Seward Hiltner, and other prominent pastoral theologians.

The revised correlational method continues to be a popular and useful method in pastoral theology, because it allows dialogue between different disciplines including literature, history, anthropology, psychology, and so forth. It also allows for the recognition that theological values have a legitimate place in evaluating the norms and values of its conversation partners. And likewise, these same conversation partners have a voice in keeping theology accountable for, at the very least, continued conversation.[2]

The nature of the dialogue between psychology and theology is especially critical in the field of pastoral theology, because, frankly, psychology has been so helpful with the everyday tasks of counseling. But there is always a concern of how to relate the truth claims of each discipline.[3]

The pastoral theological method employed here draws on the wisdom of pastoral counseling as a caring ministry of the church where the truth claims of psychology and other social sciences are drawn upon, but these claims are evaluated from the standpoint of certain norms of faith. This is to say that theology can raise certain questions of psychology; for example, Is it possible for a person to go through a spiritual transformation when all the psychological prerequisites are not in place? Cues for evaluating psychology are taken from the method of Don S. Browning and David Tracy.[4]

In this chapter a revised correlational method will be used to look at the literary work of Ernest Gaines. This method raises critical theological questions about the nature of human beings. Answers to these questions will involve the contextualization of race and sexual orientation from the viewpoint of a narrative perspective. This perspective views human nature within the dialectical tension of being good and being flawed.

Humans are a complex mix of positive motives including the best of all possible intentions as well as some of the most self-destructive human self-interests. These good intentions and self-sabotaging tendencies unfold within a teleological and purposeful narrative plot. The narrative is a faith story that gives ultimate significance and meaning to human existence.

Despite the presence of growth-destroying tendencies in our lives, present with the positive growth possibilities, it is the power of grace that holds the self-destructive dimensions in our lives in check and enables us to fulfill God's calling on our lives. The apostle Paul helps provide the theological basis for the ability of grace to manage the internal warfare going on within us. He says:

> For I know that nothing good dwells within me, that is, in my flesh. I can will what is right, but I cannot do it. For I do not do the good I want, but the evil I do not want is what I do. Now if I do what I do not want, it is no longer I that do it, but sin that dwells within me. (Romans 7:18-20)

Paul continues:

> For I delight in the law of God, in my inmost self, but I see in my mem-
> bers another law at war with the law of my mind, making me captive to
> the law of sin that dwells in my members. Wretched man that I am!
> Who will rescue me from this body of death? Thanks be to God through
> Jesus Christ our Lord! So then, with my mind I am slave to the law of
> God, but with my flesh I am slave to the law of sin. (Romans 7:22-25)

Undergirding grace is an eschatological narrative where the negative
things that happen to us and the negative things that are at work in our
lives are transformed into something positive. The negatives lose hold of
our lives, and we began to make the kinds of hopeful choices that fulfill
our lives. We began to privilege those positive conversations and stories
that enrich our lives, and we revise those conversations and stories that
lock us into bondage. Thus, the fact that we struggle with self-destructive
conversations does not doom us. Rather, the unfolding story of God's
grace in our lives leads us to transformation and growing toward the
image of God within us.

The key issue is how persons are affirmed in their value, worth, and
dignity despite the conflicting tensions within themselves as well as in
culture. Cultural definitions of what it means to be human inform many
of the public conversations that take place in the wider society. As mentioned in the last chapter, in a market-driven economy human worth and
value are based on commodification. In such a system, honor and shame
are viewed as limited commodities; honor is reserved for only the most
valued and shame for the least, last, and lost. When the Bible quotes Jesus
as saying that we should serve the least of these, he is saying that there is
honor in ministering to those persons society finds shameful. This attitude puts people who follow the teachings of Jesus in direct opposition to
current marketing values.

Likewise, conversation with God counters the commodification of
human worth, because it engages the person with a partner, God, who
conveys a sense of unlimited worth and value to the person. God makes
available to each person unlimited grace as revealed in Jesus Christ. God
offers a grace that not only will not let us go, but that provides the unlimited power of love. This love heals, guides, sustains, and reconciles such
that persons can then reach out unselfishly *to others*.

Not only is there a conversation about the commodification of human
worth, there is also a conversation about human worth based on race and

skin color. Such conversation is based on labels that assign to certain activities. For example, African Americans are given different negative labels for criminal behavior than those given to white criminals. Labels like animal are assigned more often.

A Lesson Before Dying

At the beginning of Gaines's book *A Lesson Before Dying*,[5] Jefferson is an animal. He can scarcely be called a person because he lives by animal instinct alone. He preys upon the weak, takes what he wants, and satisfies himself whenever and with whatever he can. In Jefferson's life there is no room for compassion, mercy, or commitment unless they suit his immediate needs. But through some remarkable interventions, we see the metamorphosis of this animal into a man, and not just any man, but a man who successfully imitates the attitude of Jesus. For Gaines what gives a human being value and worth is being a valued member of a faith community. This community of faith is firmly grounded in a narrative that is alive with both ancient and contemporary characters with which a person can identify. These characters are an integral part of the scenes and roles that make up the various plots. Moreover, this community teaches its members to look, even outside the church, for the God-given worth and value of all people.

Jefferson was sentenced to death by an all-white jury in Louisiana for being in the wrong place at the wrong time doing something very stupid. According to his own story, he had hitched a ride with two men who were, as it turned out, on their way to commit armed robbery at a neighborhood store. He claimed that he had no idea about their motives; he protested that he was just along for the ride. Shortly after they picked him up, he said, they stopped the car. He just waited, but it seemed that they were taking a long time. So, he went in the store to see what was going on. When he walked in, he saw blood and dead bodies on the floor. He recognized his two car acquaintances and figured that the other body was probably the store manager. Apparently, something went drastically wrong. Then he saw the money. Nobody was going to need that, so he took it. And that is what convicted him—he was caught with the stolen money.

Given racial prejudice and his background, no one believed Jefferson's story. It was just too easy for the court to believe he got greedy and shot his accomplices after they had shot and robbed the manager. Following a guilty verdict that surprised no one, Jefferson was sentenced to death. The judge pronounced the scathing remarks that Jefferson was just a scavenging hog whose only concern was an opportunity to eat the leftovers for which he didn't work.

But Jefferson's godmother was in the courtroom too. She was appalled by what the judge said. Jefferson may be many things, but he was certainly more than an animal—at least he could be. If he had to die, she resolved, he would die with dignity, not as a hog, but as fully human. The next question was how to make it happen. Jefferson's godmother and her friend enlisted the help of a young African American teacher. Mr. Wiggin had been a bright student in the local one-room schoolhouse, so bright that the community promised that they would send him away to college if he would promise to return to teach. None of them had any idea how long Jefferson's transformation would take, but they knew Mr. Wiggin had to try.

To give the reader a sense of Jefferson's transformation from his own perspective, Gaines uses a particular, but well-known literary device—a book within a book. This inner book is Jefferson's small notebook that was given to him by Mr. Wiggin. Jefferson is also given a small pencil; the head jailer is given a penknife to keep Jefferson's pencil sharp. This diary of sorts is discovered after his execution.

Jefferson's writing reflects his rudimentary education. He uses no capital letters or punctuation marks. Each word and sentence is written without spacing. Yet, from these humble origins, complex feelings arise.

Jefferson's notebook details two important things. The first is that people cared for him—the children in the one-room schoolhouse, his godmother, the pastor of the church, Mr. Wiggin, the jailers, and others. It seemed to him that everyone in his community wanted him to die like a human being rather than like an animal. They loved and accepted him.

The second thing occurred when Jefferson stopped ignoring Mr. Wiggin and started engaging him in conversation. He and Mr. Wiggin talked about God and Jesus, and as a result, the Jesus who "did not utter a mumbling word" became his role model. Through these conversations Jesus became a real source of comfort and inspiration to help him face impending death.

As Jefferson listened to the faith stories told by Mr. Wiggin, the pastor, the children who visited him en mass, and his godmother, he began to change. Through these stories he came to know that he could face death with a purpose. His death did not have to be pointless. It would in no way be like slaughtering an animal. Jefferson came to realize that his life and death mattered, maybe not to everyone, but to those that mattered to him. Just as Jesus faced execution on a cross, he too would face execution. He could do it like Jesus with faith, courage, and assurance. And that is how Jefferson did die. While his loved ones watched the execution with terror, they also saw a man face his death with composure and a sense of peace.

Toward an Understanding of Theological Anthropology

Part of the revised correlational method of pastoral theology is to evaluate answers that secular thinkers give to profound theological questions. Here we will examine Gaines's answer to the question, What does it mean to be a human being?

In Gaines's book there are two competing conversations going on. This first represents a common view during the racial climate of the pre–civil rights era. African Americans were seen as less than human. Not surprisingly this definition of what it meant to be an African American was part of the bitter fruits of slavery where persons were bought and sold as animals; they were valued and evaluated as animals. To the judge and jury Jefferson proved himself worthless when he committed his crime. He just showed them what they already knew, that he was an animal that needed to be put out of its misery—for his own good and for the good of all that surrounded him. Likewise, Jefferson easily bought into the notion that he was an animal. When the judge called him a hog, Jefferson believed him.

Jefferson may have been a criminal; he may have been low down and dirty, but he was not an animal. He was a person. True, the image of God in Jefferson was scarred beyond recognition, but that did not mean that it was irredeemable. Jefferson's community wanted Jefferson to reclaim that image before he died. So Jefferson's godmother and other friends, including several prison officials, labored to find that image of God within Jefferson and to bring it into the light. Only then would Jefferson have the choice to become a person of faith able to reflect God's power and peace to others.

The Caring Community

For Gaines, being human means being vitally connected to a caring community. A caring community has as its central task the guidance and nurture of persons into their full development as human beings. The caring community has to be firmly grounded in a spiritual or faith tradition, although not all members will ever be at the same level of faith. To be rich in caring, communities must also have an abundance of active symbols that impact persons' lives. Ideally, a caring community needs the wisdom of different generations, interacting in full participation so that meaning may be continually transformed and transmitted to others.

The conversations offered by caring communities are different from those of the wider society. The community's conversations reflect the fundamental value and universal worth of all people. In caring communities relationships and relationship building are primary, and the commodification of persons is discouraged.

Unfortunately for Jefferson, he grew up cut off from a caring community. He seemed to have only acquaintances that were his peers. The experience of having another person put self-interest aside for him was foreign. Before he could recover God's image within himself, he had to be loved into a caring community. In Gaines's book we see how a person must be loved first before he or she can love back. Then once love is operative, one's image of God can be salvaged to again develop and eventually flourish. One must be a vital part of a caring community for transformation to occur.

Gaines made the setting for Jefferson's transformation the prison cell. One does not have to be outside the prison walls to be free enough to find God's gift of personhood. The caring community can come into the prison, and this is what happened to Jefferson. The prison cell became a crucible for God's care through a community of faith. A crucible is a pot into which materials are put and then heated to a very high temperature. In crucibles of various kinds gold is refined and steel is forged. Whatever is heated in the crucible comes out transformed. A prison cell can be a crucible as can the human heart where the fire of love ignites to transform persons into new and better conversation partners with God.

Even though Jefferson is in a prison cell, Gaines shows how Jefferson is enabled to internalize caring relationships so that he *can* encounter religious and spiritual values through significant conversations. But as the notebook informs us, Jefferson was not passively nurtured into the community life. He took an active part to critically evaluate his own inner conversations about himself as an animal and as a human. Which is better? Which way should he go? What does Jesus say? As he opens himself through questions such as these, he is also making room to hear God's voice and engage God in conversation.

Jefferson's diary records the events of his transformation. While there are many, several stand out. The first is his dream that foretells of his transformation. One way to look at this is to see his unconscious mind entertaining the possibility of change—a kind of "what would it be like if . . . ?" Another way to look at his dream is to understand that the hidden and obscured image of God was awakening. Yet, Jefferson didn't understand his dream, because he still thought of himself as a hog.[6] In fact, while he was dreaming, he had a hard time understanding why they didn't just take him out and kill him like a hog rather than putting him to death in the electric chair.

About the same time as the dream, Jefferson had a visit from Mr. Wiggin. Although Mr. Wiggin was not a practitioner of his faith, Jefferson began asking about Good Friday and Easter. The more Jefferson learned about Jesus, the more he made a connection between his death and Jesus' death. The fact that Jesus died without saying a "mumbling word," was somehow meaningful to Jefferson.

The third milestone happened as Jefferson was reunited with children. His diary recorded the time when a child reached out and gave him a marble as a gift. At that moment he realized that he belonged, that he was loved and cared for. Being shown love by the children gave Jefferson the resolve to face death courageously for others. Here was a place that Jefferson could be like Jesus. He too would save little children who would not only know his story, but be shaped by his witness. He would give them a lesson on how to live in the face of dying. Thus, through the eyes of children, Jefferson finally knew his mission and purpose in life.

The point to be made here about theological anthropology is that it is possible to affirm one's own essential humanity while one's own existence is imminently threatened. One's meaning and value can be affirmed even as one faces death. For Jefferson, the crucible of the prison cell was all about evaluating all the conversations about what it meant to be human. What emerged from the white-hot heat of love was a new Jefferson, a person of purpose, conviction, and compassion.

Evaluating Gaines's Image of Full Humanity

Gaines gives us two kinds of answers to what it means to be human. The first answer is in the form of a definition of what it means to be human, and the second is a description of a process for human transformation. In this section, the objective is to evaluate both answers as we move toward understanding pastoral counseling as a crucible for the formation of sacred identity.

Theologically African American Christianity focuses centrally on the person of Jesus. In his book, Gaines too focuses on the person of Jesus, specifically on the Jesus of the cross. Given this emphasis, perhaps we can say that Gaines implies the Jesus of the resurrection. In any case it is identification with Jesus that shifts Jefferson's conversation to what it means to be fully human, in other words, not an animal. Jefferson learns that being fully human means giving oneself to others. Being human means being an engaged and valued member of a caring community that makes contributions to the growth of both self and others in relation. In this sense, Gaines follows a long-standing Christian theological tradition that allows human character to be shaped by the life and death of Jesus. Jefferson is transformed into a hero because, in the end, he, like Jesus, becomes the kind of human being that gives his life for the lives of others.

Although there is no indication that Jefferson is ever baptized or confirmed in the faith, he is nevertheless transformed, at least according to the author, into an imitator of Christ. There is every sense that Jesus does save Jefferson. From reading Gaines's other books, particularly *In My Father's House*, one can see his uneasiness with the institutional church. This unease is exemplified in *A Lesson Before Dying* by Mr. Wiggin who as a nonpracticing Christian leads Jefferson through transformation. Mr. Wiggin contrasts with the minister, with whom Jefferson never develops a relationship. I think that Gaines wanted to make a significant contrast between the love and care of a secular person and the aloofness of a Christian professional. Interestingly enough, even this contrast has religious echoes to the good Samaritan story as told in the gospel by Jesus. If Gaines is offering a critique of institutionalized religion, he stands in good company.

From the vantage point of the theological concept of grace, Gaines's theology of human development is close to Paul Tillich's theology of acceptance. For Tillich sin is estrangement from God, and God's forgive-ness is made manifest in God's acceptance of humans. Acceptance is then being affirmed at the core of one's being as valued by God.[7] God also gave Jefferson the power to transcend his past and live by Jesus' power as he faced death courageously. Using the language of Paul Tillich, Jefferson then had the courage to *be*. He was united with his essential humanity and thus transformed. Using the language of John Wesley, Jefferson renounced the spiritual forces of wickedness, rejected the evil powers of this world, and repented of his sin. He accepted the freedom and power of God to resist evil, injustice, and oppression. In short, Jefferson repented and accepted the justifying and sanctifying grace of the Holy Spirit.

A crucible, to reiterate, is a context, place, or a setting where diverse conversations of what it means to be human are discovered, explored, sorted through, and refined in the heat of interpersonal relationship. Relationships are always central to the process of making meaning. In Gaines's work, the prison cell became the crucible, but in a sense any place of bondage can itself become a crucible. Any place where human growth and transformation are thwarted is a prison, but the good news is that God is able to help persons transcend the chains of bondage even from within the darkest, deepest prison. Through God's prevenient grace, seeds can be planted and nurtured through the caring community. In the midst of human suffering at its worst, the prison cell can become a moth-ering cocoon where conversation with God can be transformative.

In the book Jefferson's godmother and the elders become the human pressure that stoke the fires of the crucible. Cross-generational visitors, including children and prison guards, become new conversation partners. From these affirming conversations, conversation with God becomes more than a possibility. These human conversations help open Jefferson to the possibility of, to use William James, "the will to believe." Through conversation Jefferson begins to hear that he can be different and he can make a difference. He begins to understand that God made him in God's image and as such, he is a child of God. The old conversations that held fears of being an abandoned orphan are replaced with new conversations that are full of acceptance and nurture. Once Jefferson gets this taste of love, he feeds from its nourishment until he begins to look for its divine source. His *real self* that had been dormant begins to awaken. His *false self*, the hog, as the court had labeled it, begins to whither away. Slowly even his physical countenance changes.

A Psychosocial Analysis

The revised correlational method also suggests that theology can examine and benefit from the input of behavioral science. This section will draw on some insights that Erik Erikson had about black identity in 1964. For him, the self-understanding of youth about their place in society and their potential contribution to society needed concrete affirmation through the promise of future work or vocation. For example, Erikson pointed out that there were three conversations in wider culture about the roles African American youth were to play in wider society. These roles included servants of whites, educated professionals who knew their place, and societal misfits who could be put in prison if they stepped out of line.

The social roles that Jefferson played so successfully have a long legacy in this country. Being a criminal and particularly an African American criminal are social roles in our society. These roles arise in part out of racism. In our society racism is about crippling the ability of a group of people so that they become the scapegoats for the problems of another group. It is about recruiting persons into destructive stories not of their own creation. Through limiting available choices and reinforcing specific choices, persons are subtly encouraged to play the role of a scapegoat. Erik Erikson made this observation in his monumental study of black identity, *Childhood and Society*.[8]

Jefferson needed very little encouragement to become a criminal; he seemed to find comfort in internalizing that role. It gave him a sense of identity, a set of comrades, and rules of engagement. He mastered the language and values that enabled him to meet his survival needs. The problem was that once he had so subscribed to that role, subscribing to other social roles became problematic. The negative conversations into which he was recruited cut off the possibility of entering into any other kind. To find an alternative conversation that might give him the opportunity to develop another identity or take another social role became impossible. Hence, Jefferson was in bondage long before he went to prison.

The prison cell becomes the locus where Jefferson begins to encounter alternative conversations of what it means to be human. As he encounters diverse definitions, he begins to reflect and to think about them. Then as he sorts through the different alternatives, his true self begins to emerge. Just as Jefferson finds in the prison cell the freedom to explore the many images and meanings of being human, persons can find pastoral counseling an analogous context. One of the goals of pastoral counseling is to explore a variety of social images of what it means to be human. Within the caring context of pastoral counseling, cultural images are compared and critiqued. Because crisis often motivates persons to seek counseling, the counseling session can easily become a crucible for change. If persons stick around long enough to work through and past the crisis, counseling can also become a context for transformation.

The work of Ernest Gaines can give us some clues for how to develop a theory of pastoral counseling as a crucible for the sacred. To understand one's self as a child of God is the beginning of one's sacred identity formation. As such, one's sacred identity involves centering or privileging one's self-worth in the gift of conversation with God. Pastoral counseling is a relational context that values religious conversation and sacred identity formation in the lives of individuals and groups of people within the larger communities of faith. Pastoral counseling can also be an affirming environment in which various conversations can be explored and evaluated despite unfavorable or unproductive cultural conversations.

Gaines's work points to the importance of affirmation from a relational context. In his book, Gaines suggests a community of faith can be one context; I am suggesting that pastoral counseling can be another such context. To paraphrase the Bible, we love because God first loves us. Wesley's theological interpretation of the biblical truth is prevenient grace; what Gaines adds is that we love because the community of faith first loves us. That is to say that sometimes people are so enmeshed in destructive conversations, sometimes people feel so shamed, and sometimes people are so hurt, that it takes the caring community of faith to remove barriers so that God's grace might be experienced. I am saying that pastoral counseling can be a manifestation of the caring community.

Often in pastoral counseling broken people come for healing and guidance, but their very brokenness is itself an obstacle to experience the care of the caregiver. People come straining to hear the voice of God, but they are, for example, afraid of God (as they understand God) or of what they might have to do if they do hear God's voice; so they try to use the counselor as a go-between. Many pastoral counselors have the experience of persons projecting their image of God on the counselor. While this may be a step in the process toward conversation with God for the person, it can be very conflicting if the counselee has a negative image of God. The pastoral counselor may experience some negative countertransference.

Reflecting on people's lives who have come for pastoral counseling has taught me an important lesson. Object relations psychology talks about several key needs that people have and that need satisfaction. The basic idea is that human beings become persons of worth when they are surrounded by people, with positive attitudes, who can be internalized. Such positive persons become enduring sources of nurture and self-esteem when internalized. From a religious point of view, having internalized positive significant others also enables us to engage God. Satisfying the basic needs for positive internalized others frees us to turn our attention to God, the ultimate source of worth. Internalized frustrating relationships with others often prevent us from turning our attention to God since these internalized others selfishly demand our full attention.

Merle Jordan in his insightful book *Taking on the Gods: The Task of the Pastoral Counselor* makes the point that internalized frustrating others block our relationship with God. This is because internalized frustrating relationships become idols that demand our worship, and as such prevent us from investing psychic energy in God.[9] Through the visits of others to the jail, Jefferson had an opportunity to internalize positive others who then became inner sources of self-esteem and strength. He then had the internalized voices and conversations to counter the other negative inner conversations. When those positive persons, voices, and conversations took root, he was then able to hear God's voice talking to him as well. The older inner voices that sabotaged self-esteem were silenced.

Symbolism

In Gaines's book, Jefferson anchored his worth in the figure of Christ on the cross. This image of Christ came to symbolize who Jefferson could be, and he identified closely with it. Symbolization is the process where images come to persons from the depths of the mind. These images can then become potential sources of new self-understandings.[10] The self seems to be constituted at the symbolic level first through the spontaneous appearances of images that come from the depths of the subconscious life. These symbols are called primary symbols and always require some interpretation by the person.[11] This emergence of primary symbols can be triggered by a variety of factors including ritual and discourse. Reflecting on these images as they emerge assists in a person's identity formation because they are essential dimensions of the self emerging for exploration. This reflection on the image for the purposes of establishing implications for identity formation is called secondary symbolization. Finally, tertiary symbolization is the establishment of the source of images in the appropriate narrative to confirm the source of identity.

Primary symbolization takes place when images or ideas make their sudden appearance in our awareness. Often this happens when there is a significant dream that we might have. We don't understand its meaning at first, but it remains on our minds and hearts waiting to be interpreted and for implications to be made for our everyday lives.

Often we engage others in helping us to explore the meaning of these emergent images or ideas. We enter into various conversations in attempts to discern significance. When we enter into these deciphering conversations, we have entered the phase of secondary symbolization. We are eliciting the help of others in the interpretation of the erupted image or idea.

Finally, the meaning of the image, idea, or dream crystallizes in our minds. Often this crystallizing of meaning is connected to a story or narrative plot that provides added meaning and significance to our lives. The plot links many unrelated aspects together to form a meaningful whole that gives perspective to where we currently are in our lives. This third level of significance is called tertiary symbolization.

The three movements of symbolization can be clearly seen in Gaines's work, *A Lesson Before Dying*. First, the image of Jesus dying on the cross surfaces. Second, Jefferson seeks to explore the significance of this image for his own life on death row. Third, the image is linked to the Christian story of the life, death, and resurrection of Jesus Christ.

By understanding symbolization in this way, it is possible to visualize another way pastoral counseling can become a crucible for sacred identity formation. When an individual is ready to shift inner conversations from dominant cultural images, appropriate new images can emerge. These new images can become the grist for new conversations. As the person begins to shift through and reflect on these new conversations, they can be explored. Then through the exploration process, the true self becomes clearer, emerging, as it were, from the depths into the light of consciousness. The images are then woven into the faith narrative opening the possibility of further conversations with significant others (especially God), conversations that can be internalized to become part of the person's identity.

As a result, the person has a new sense of personal worth and value that in turn results in the person seeing others with an enhanced sense of their worth and value. Pastoral counseling can function through the same three movements of symbolization. First, there is the emergence of primary symbols. Second, there is the exploration of these symbols for self-development. Third, these symbols can be linked to the larger faith stories and can serve as new conversation partners. However, this stage is not complete until the ensuing transformation results in the person seeing increased worth and value of others in the community. Thus through the process of symbolization, conversation with God can hold a privileged place in the person's self-understanding.

Significance of Symbolization for Pastoral Counseling

Symbolization is always a part of the pastoral counseling process. As counselors we need to be patient and create a space for the primary symbols to emerge. Our theology suggests that God's presence will be made known in the counseling process. God's presence will not remain hidden. As religious professionals, we need to be ready to receive God's revelation, because when it happens, both the pastoral counselor and the counselee will begin the secondary and tertiary symbolization processes.

Job's experience is instructive for pastoral counseling at this point. In chapter 13 of the book of Job, Job forcefully declares the priority of conversation with God above all other conversations. It is significant that Job decides that no matter what his pain, he has to directly confront God, even if it means death. Job shows remarkable courage in speaking to God so forcefully, since such a confrontation would be viewed as blasphemy by his culture. Therefore, he risked confrontation with God not knowing the outcome. Thus, the writer of Job was setting the stage for introducing lament as a basic form of communication with God that was not viewed as blasphemy. Rather, lament emerged as a pursuit of God rather than as an affront to God. Job's faith is manifest in his certainty that his life is in the hands of God. Job's hopes lies in God's righteousness and God's faithfulness, but Job also knows that God can choose to let him die. Nevertheless, Job determines to let no other conversations come before conversation with God. He says to his friends:

> Your maxims are proverbs of ashes,
> your defenses are defenses of clay.

Let me have silence, and I will speak,
and let come on me what may.
I will take my flesh in my teeth,
and put my life in my hand.
See, he will kill me; I have no hope;
but I will defend my ways to his face.
This will be my salvation,
that the godless shall not come before him.
Listen carefully to my words,
and let my declaration be in your ears.
I have indeed prepared my case;
I know that I shall be vindicated.

(Job 13:12-18)

From Job's experience pastoral counselors can see that privileging God conversation is a process. Even when God's presence appears to be hidden, there are glimpses of hope that God might reveal God's self even in the midst of dread and deep anxiety. We see in Job another example of what Tillich calls the courage to be. It is in the courage to take our vulnerability before God that we can truly encounter God's presence. Despite Job's woundedness, he is willing to be open enough to enter into direct conversation with God. This gives him hope.[12]

Many counselees who come for pastoral counseling would not feel as free as Job to engage God with that courage. In this context, pastoral counselors need to provide the warmth and security for the counselee to enter into God conversation. Many counselees don't come to pastoral counseling with the inner strength to enter God conversation, and they must develop this capacity through pastoral counseling.

Pastoral counselors need patience along with expectation. Patience refers to the need to trust God's hiddenness within the counseling process. Yet, we still need the expectation that God's presence will manifest itself. We need to have faith in God's steadfast love and grace.

Expectation is driven by memory, both the memory of what God has done in the lives of individuals and what God has done in the lives of God's representative communities as recorded in the Bible. We have hope because we understand that Job's conversations and confrontation with God are possibilities for each of us in the here and now. The expectations of such possibilities are part of God's gracious promise of God's presence in the midst of life. God is always a faithful conversation partner, eager to draw us into conversation with God and to enable us to engage in meaningful conversation with others.

Symbolization and mimetic repetition are related. Patterns and structures of past meaning help us form expectations of the future. The life, death, and resurrection of Jesus can be viewed as an archetypal and repetitive pattern that continues to offer us the hope of transformation. As God's unfolding story of transformation continues, we can become a part of God's narrative. We, like Jefferson, can recognize that we are more than animals. We are valuable children of God who can love others.

Notes

1. Ernest J. Gaines, *A Lesson Before Dying* (New York: Vintage Books, 1994).

2. David Tracy believes that truth claims are made in every field of inquiry, but he believed these truth claims should not go unchallenged by appeal to traditional religious authority as in the case of theology. See Alan Richardson and John Bowde, eds., *The Westminster Dictionary of Christian Theology* (Philadelphia: Westminster Press, 1983), 364-65.

3. See Seward Hiltner, *Preface to Pastoral Theology: The Ministry and Theory of Shepherding* (Nashville: Abingdon Press, 1958), 20-21.

4. Don S. Browning, *Religious Thought and the Modern Psychologies: A Critical Conversation in the Theology of Culture* (Philadelphia: Fortress Press, 1987).

5. Gaines, *A Lesson Before Dying*.

6. Ibid., 220.

7. Paul Tillich, *Systematic Theology*, Vol. 2 (Chicago: University of Chicago Press, 1957), 1178-79.

8. Erik Erikson, *Childhood and Society* (New York: W. W. Norton, 1963), 241-46.

9. Merle R. Jordan, *Taking on the Gods: The Task of the Pastoral Counselor* (Nashville: Abingdon Press, 1986), 21-39.

10. This understanding of symbolization comes from two different but related sources. The first is from the exploration of the images that appear in the conversion experiences of African Americans who survived slavery. See Edward P. Wimberly and Anne Streaty Wimberly, *Liberation and Human Wholeness: The Conversion Experiences of Black People in Slavery and Freedom* (Nashville: Abingdon Press, 1986), 15-22. The second source is Paul Ricoeur, *The Symbolism of Evil* (Boston: Beacon Press, 1967), 9-10.

11. Ricoeur, *Symbolism of Evil*, 9.

12. J. Gerald Janzen point out that it is courage of absolute vulnerability that enables Job to take his fears before God. This fosters trust in God. See *Job, Interpretation: A Bible Commentary for Teaching and Preaching* (Atlanta: John Knox Press, 1985), 107-8.

CHAPTER THREE

SACRED IDENTITY FORMATION AND SEXUALITY

In the previous chapter we talked about Ernest J. Gaines's book, *A Lesson Before Dying*. Gaines introduces us to a character named Jefferson who comes to identify closely with Jesus on the cross. Jefferson develops a sacred identity despite having no discernible childhood experience in a faith community. But a faith community does step forward to embrace Jefferson, and it is this faith community that reaches out to him in prison and ushers him toward finding his sacred worth and value as a beloved child of God. Gaines's work illustrates a theological fact—God's activity is not limited to working just within the confines of the church. God is never left without a credible witness.

This chapter explores the nature of sacred identity formation among those who acknowledge themselves to be homosexual. The major theological question here is, What is sacred identity formation like for a person when the dominant conversations about one's worth and value are negative? E. Lynn Harris attempts to answer this question.

E. Lynn Harris is a contemporary African American novelist whose main characters are struggling with what it means to be homosexual and bisexual in contemporary American and African American society. He views himself as a born-again Christian, and he gives spirituality a central place in the lives of his characters. Based on the six books I have read by Harris, his significance is that he gives us real glimpses of the intimate, personal, emotional, and spiritual lives of people who are struggling with their sexual identities. He has much to teach us about the formation of sacred identity among homosexuals and bisexuals.

Contemporary Conversation About Homosexuality

In our market-driven economy, we are recruited into conversations that serve the marketplace. From these various conversations, personal and group psychological identities form. The values that our society promotes are exemplified by the self-contained, self-actualized, independent person. As described by the market economy, an autonomous person is free from relational entanglements in order to pursue consumer goods in an unencumbered way.

Often in our society unencumbered also means disconnected. It is as though the more disconnected a person is, the more individualistic he or she seems; and hence society views that person as strong and powerful. Our society glorifies and creates myths about the individual who takes on the world alone, or the person who achieves success against all odds. However, in reality being disconnected from significant others in community makes a person weaker and impotent, not stronger or powerful. One has only to take a long look at the history of African Americans. Slaves were routinely torn from their families. As a result , many lacked the benefit and nurture of a consistent caring community. Yet, there is abundant evidence that many intact black families survived slavery, because they recognized the significance of cross-generational connections.[1]

Being a disconnected or unencumbered individual is constantly reinforced by a public morality that supports achievement outside the home—in the jungle, as the workplace is often described. We even call looking for a job, job hunting. The image is of a lone (male) hunter armed with the values of competition, fortitude, courage, resourcefulness, and perseverance. Even the term "market driven" is telling. We never say that we nurture the market. Rather the market is driven and hence drives us by mysterious market forces that appear elemental as well as transcendent. Not only that, but survival of the fittest is a common business strategy.

Market values prop up the bottom line with profitability often at any cost while eschewing the virtues of sacrifice, commitment, or care unless these virtues show themselves as the allies of financial success. Sacrifice is fine as long as it is in service to the bottom line. Commitment is fine as long as it is in homage to the bottom line. According to Sylvia Ann Hewlett and Cornel West, "In the late 1990's what really counts in America is how much you get paid and what you can buy."[2] Not surprisingly, commitment to the job often conflicts with commitment to significant others, including family.

Accompanying the emphasis on the autonomous individual is a corresponding emphasis on the libertine philosophy of privacy in one's personal life, particularly as it relates to sexual behavior. Despite the fact that society often says that consenting adult individuals can do what they want in the privacy of their own home (in the realm of adult sexual behavior), society also often undermines persons' inner freedom to be what they are, especially in the area of sexual identity.

Traditionally, human worth and value are linked to being heterosexual. By and large, this has not changed in our contemporary climate. Theologically, it is my view that both heterosexual and homosexual persons are worthwhile and valued by God. Self-worth is a gift from God bestowed without regard to meritorious sexual activity on our part. This view is ancient, having roots in Christian theology. For example, Richard Hays points out that biblically there is no essential gender orientation. He says: "Nowhere does the Bible speak of sexual orientation, nor does it categorize the identity of human beings according to their sexual preferences. The tendency to describe sexual orientation as a fundamental 'hard-wired' aspect of personhood is a modern development."[3]

Because essential human identity is not based on sexual orientation, Hays says, "there are numerous homosexual Christians whose lives show signs of the presence of God, whose work in ministry is genuine and effective." He says that "God gives the Spirit to broken people and ministers grace even through us sinners without endorsing our sin."[4] Hays helps us visualize that God's grace is universally available to all, regardless of our sexual orientation.

E. Lynn Harris embraces this universality of grace in his novels. He affirms that human worth and value are gifts bestowed by God on persons regardless of sexual orientation. This is especially the case in his novels, *Abide With Me* and *Just As I Am*.[5] Harris identifies himself as a born-again Christian and as a self-avowed gay person. As in the case of Ernest Gaines, E. Lynn Harris's books are excellent studies in sacred identity formation. His works give insight into the working of God's gifts of identity and worth, despite one's sexual orientation. His novels help many gay and lesbian persons overcome the way our culture recruits them into negative and demeaning identities. In our society being gay or lesbian carries strong negative values despite our marketing emphasis on privacy.

In this chapter we will explore what E. Lynn Harris has to teach us about the crucibles for sacred identity formation. For him, human worth and value can be confirmed by God through a mystical encounter with one of God's divine agents. He uses this kind of encounter to show how, after a long struggle, one's sexual preference is confirmed as part of one's total self-worth.[6]

The fact that Harris rests his notion of identity clearly in relationship with God, rather than in one's sexuality, puts him at odds with some self-affirming gay Christian groups. For example, Richard Hays makes this point by referring to a colleague who was dying of AIDS, but who was angry with self-affirming groups because they denied the complex and tragic dimension of homosexuality. Hays's dying friend said that gay apologists "encouraged homosexual believers to 'draw their identity from their sexuality' and thus to shift the ground of their identity subtly and idolatrously away from God."[7] While he makes it very clear that sexuality is part of one's identity, he also makes it clear that one's identity transcends one's sexuality. In other words, he does not ground human identity in either biology or human relationships, but rather in a relationship with God. Harris's great contribution is to help us envision how negative identities can be overcome, especially for gay and lesbian persons.

Toward Sacred Identity Formation

In his book *Abide With Me*, Harris sets forth his view that sacred worth is a gift bestowed by God. This book concludes when one of the characters, Raymond Tyler, has a theophany. He encounters an angel, Kyle, from heaven. Kyle, while living on earth, was a homosexual who died of

AIDS. Raymond is a homosexual in a committed homosexual relationship. God chooses Kyle to give Raymond a message that both affirms and confirms his life, including his sexual orientation.

The setting of the divine revelation is a football stadium. Raymond stands alone, gathering his thoughts, as snow falls from the sky. He is thinking of his parents and the current illness of his father. Unsure of what to do about his estrangement from his father, Raymond also begins thinking about his sometimes unfaithful partner. His thoughts wander, and he thinks about his profession as well. Cold and alone, Raymond lets the snow begin to cover him.

In the midst of his thoughts Raymond sees a man crossing the field, coming in his direction. At first Raymond is resentful, thinking that his much-needed solitude is about to be interrupted. The man moves swiftly toward Raymond and stands with him before he can respond. At first Raymond does not recognize who this person is; then he sees it is his old friend Kyle—who is dead. Even so, Raymond hugs his friend. "What are you doing here? I thought you were dead."[8] Trying to recover, Raymond still can't quite believe what is happening. "Perhaps I am going crazy," he thinks. The reunion serves, however, to make him realize just how lonely he really is, and he begins to cry uncontrollably.

Kyle is dressed all in white, looking much younger. There is a glow about him. Kyle confirms that Raymond is having a dream, but no ordinary dream—a dream sent by God.[9] Kyle also confirms that he is there to help. The purpose of Kyle's visit is to give Raymond a message. Before hearing the message, Raymond has a vision of a white house with an evergreen wreath on the door. On the porch there is a green swing. Snow is falling everywhere. Jungian psychology would suggest Raymond's vision is a symbol of new birth.[10]

The message that Kyle gives Raymond deals with Raymond's fears and anxieties about his ill father. It is a message of comfort, but it also contains the assurance that his father really loves him. Kyle also gives Raymond some advice about how to handle his partner. Kyle says for Raymond not to put his ultimate faith in his partner, but in "our heavenly Father and yourself. Don't worry, you'll never be alone."[11]

As peace comes over Raymond and his worries lift, Kyle gives one more admonition: to stop listening to the rain and listen only to the snow, "That silent voice you hear when you are totally alone, where there are no media, bosses, father, mother, brother, or lovers telling you what you should do. When you listen to the voice of snow, it will never lead you wrong. It will make a difference in your life."[12]

Now Raymond knows for sure that there is a God and a heaven. So he decides to take another step; he asks Kyle what heaven is like. In heaven, Kyle says, one can hear the snow.[13] In the language of this book, heaven is a place where God's voice is clearly heard and where there are no other voices competing for center stage in a person's life.

The implied author[14] is a theologian who has something to say about identity formation and homosexuality. The process of identity formation is a gift from God, but coming to grips with one's sexual orientation is also something that must be worked out in relationship to God. Accordingly, sexual orientation is a personal and private part of one's life that can only be clarified in relationship to God. This point of view has been quite common in the African American community in times past.

Reflection on Privileging Conversation with God

In Harris's narrative Kyle brings a message from God. In talking to Raymond, Kyle becomes the voice of God confirming Raymond's value and worth. Kyle also tells Raymond to put his faith in God and in himself and to listen to the snow, the "still small voice" of God. Snow symbolizes the authentic voice of God that blankets the world. This voice can be trusted. The rain, however, is the noisy voice of the world that drowns rather than blankets. The voice of snow is comforting; the voice of rain is threatening. Listening to the snow also means that God's revelations can occur more than once, and that Raymond should expect to hear from God in the future. The affirming message for Raymond is that he is not alone in his struggles. God will see him through.

Unfortunately, Harris's book ends with this vision/dream. The reader is left to wonder what Raymond did with his message. We do know, however, that the book acknowledges the struggles and complexity that exist in relationships generally and in relationships further complicated by issues around sexual orientation specifically.

The author not only has a high regard for conversation with God but also a high regard for human friendship. Friendship with family and friends is an essential dimension of living life abundantly. Yet, the author suggests that human relationships can become idolatrous, supplanting or overshadowing relationship with God.

The character of Kyle is also interesting. Through Kyle, Harris suggests that life endures and even thrives after the suffering, pain, and confusion brought about by death. Life with God continues as an unfolding story. In a sense, then, a person's story has no ending, just as Harris's book has no proper ending. All closures are premature when persons partner with God. Hope is always available to us if we can just listen to the comforting voice of the snow. Also, in a not-so-subtle way, Harris suggests that Kyle, the homosexual angel, is not only in heaven but plays a vital role as God's messenger.

As a title, *Abide With Me* points to a notion of a present and available God who is intimately involved in human affairs. God is a historical God who draws closer to persons in times of difficulty or who sends messengers to convey specific information to keep life unfolding in meaningful ways. The God presented here is one who seeks out relationships with humans and who takes the initiative to comfort persons with a good word.

With regard to sexuality, the novel leaves open the question of sexual orientation. Kyle, God's messenger, is clearly a gay man who died of AIDS. The message is that Kyle's sexual orientation does not hinder his entrance into heaven. There is no renunciation of his gay identity, and it is clear that Kyle dies still thinking of himself as a gay person.

An interesting point, however, is Kyle's statement when he appears as an angel to Raymond. Kyle tells Raymond to trust his relationship with God above all other relationships, including one's sexual partner. God, through Kyle, affirms that there are genuine positive relationships between gay lovers, but that no relationship should be elevated to the level of God. Putting any relationship on par with God is idolatry. Trusting only in God ultimately leads to meaning.

In another novel Harris describes a situation in which God is unhappy when persons try to be someone they are not,[15] but Harris stops short of ascribing the origins of homosexuality to God. However, sexual orientation is no obstacle to God bestowing God's grace. The words "Just As I Am" seem to reflect the theology that God's grace transcends sexual orientation. God confirms our worth as human beings and offers unconditional love regardless. Thus, sacred worth is a gift from God. One is neither included nor excluded in divine conversation because of sexual orientation.

The Crucible Context

Harris's novels not only recognize the importance of giving conversation with God top priority, they also contain realistic messages about the limits of human relationships. The imagery of rain versus snow in *Abide With Me* helps lift up the author's reservations about human relationships. Rain represents horizontal or human relationships; snow symbolizes vertical or heavenly conversation. The angel as a conveyor of theological wisdom seems to communicate that all human relationships, particularly intimate ones, are suspect. They can lead one to idolatry. Although Harris describes some intimate relationships as complex and problematic, he nonetheless gives an accurate portrayal of human finitude.

The relationship between parents, especially between fathers and their gay sons is shown to be very troublesome. Raymond's relationship with his father is a good example. Through this father-son relationship Harris helps the reader explore the significance of the need to connect and reconnect with parents as part of a homosexual's or bisexual's ongoing, unfolding story. Harris uses characters such as Raymond Tyler and Basil Henderson to chart the pilgrimage toward self-acceptance that can come as a result of authentically relating with the same-sex parent. *Authentic* here refers to being truthful about one's sexual orientation and not having to hide it from one's family of origin. Harris portrays that such authentic living is possible and is something to look forward to. Thus, one's family of origin again becomes the crucible for identity formation.

While the family is one crucible for identity formation, another is psychotherapy. Harris describes psychotherapy as a place where one can explore one's sexuality and sexual orientation in an atmosphere of trust and confidentiality. Although the therapeutic context is not inviolate, it does offer a place where personal exploration and growth is possible. Another context of safe exploration Harris portrays is long-lasting groups of college friends. Harris seems to point to the fact that persons who are at odds with conventional sexual morality can find safe havens where identity can be formed and conversation with God can be cultivated.

If This World Were Mine

Harris's realistic expectations for horizontal relationships are contained most clearly in his novel entitled *If This World Were Mine*.[16] The title comes from a song made famous by a popular African American singer, Luther Vandross. The title is significant for the story because of its meaning to a small group of friends who first meet during their college days at Hampton Institute. They form a group that meets monthly to chart the progress each member makes in fulfilling their individual hopes and dreams. Each member keeps a journal and reads various selections of it at the monthly meeting.

As the group meets over time, it becomes a crucible with a collective journal of a sort. Harris's storytelling skillfully leads the reader to those things in the life of each group member that really matter. Often these things take the form of obstacles that prevent the member from achieving his or her goal or that make meaning impossible. The author helps expose unresolved past issues that prevent the individual group members from claiming their dreams and hopes in the world. Often these obstacles are described as childhood relationships that need therapeutic attention. As the individual stories of the members unfold, a series of subepisodes show how these obstacles are overcome with the help of others in the group.

The group members are straight, gay, married, and single. As they share their vulnerabilities, we the readers see how a group of friends can become an inclusive crucible for all kinds of people. We also see how each member contributes to the whole group as they hammer out trusting relationships.

An important character in this book, as well as in some of Harris's other books, is Basil Henderson. Basil is a bisexual former National League Football player who denies his homosexual tendencies. He always seems to find himself with an attractive, budding movie actress when, inevitably, his homosexual struggles surface and his relationship with the diva ends. As a child Basil was sexually molested by his uncle. While this event seems to be the source of Basil's identity issues, the story surfaces in the Hampton group as Basil tries to work out his relationship with his father. The uncle, as it turns out, was Basil's father's favorite younger brother.

As Basil confronts his tragic past, he finds himself between the proverbial rock and hard place. His latest girl friend, Yolanda, confronts him about his bisexuality which he denies. But he pleads with her, telling how his sexuality was tragically complicated and hoping that she will be sympathetic. She isn't and they break up.

In Basil's case most of the events take place outside of the group, but the members nonetheless support him. Basil's past suddenly comes to the group's center stage when his father calls Basil to tell him that his uncle has cancer and is in desperate financial need. With no medical insurance, Basil's father thinks that his financially successful former NFL football star will save the day. As it turns out, this is the very same uncle who molested Basil; and Basil refuses to help, much to the dismay, hurt, and confusion of his father.

Rather than seeking emotional escape by the usual route of bisexual encounters, Basil turns to his friend Raymond Tyler. Although not a member of the group, Basil trusts Raymond because of their history together. Raymond had been one of Basil's sexual partners, but he also knows that Raymond will keep the sexual boundaries and is a safe person with whom he can share his real concerns.

In the book we see Raymond help his friend Basil unlock the door of his past and eventually receive healing. As he lies sleeping one night, Basil has a nightmare. In the dream he sees himself lying on his bed. Right before dawn the door opens and his uncle comes in and slips into bed with him. When he awakens, Basil asks, "The memories of my childhood are coming to the surface like boiling water. But why now? I ask myself. Memories that are like Holyfield body blows. Any one of them could knock me reeling."[17] The rage that follows the emergent memories is all-consuming. He wants nothing more than for his uncle to die. Basil wants to cry, but tears will not come. He thinks, "Tears are for sissies. My uncle Mac taught me that."[18] That same uncle abused him and locked him into an inescapable psychological bind. Uncle Mac made fun of Basil for acting like a female while treating him like one.

Basil berates himself for being unable to confront his father or his uncle with the truth. In his pain, Basil calls Raymond again. Here Harris presents Raymond as a mature self-affirming mentor who happens to be homosexual. Basil and Raymond connect at a deep level with unconditional empathy. Through his actions Raymond is transformed into a therapist who has the same qualities we see in Kyle the angel. Raymond is the earthly embodiment of the angel who brought the message of joy and self-affirmation in the midst of life. Raymond and Basil connect on a human level guided by a divine vision. Raymond is able to demonstrate to Basil what God did for him when he was at his lowest.

Basil admires Raymond's close-knit family where there is love with no secrets. Because of his observations of Raymond's family, Basil believes that Raymond can offer him some wisdom. Therefore, Basil seeks out Raymond as a font of wisdom. Through their encounter, Harris shows how Raymond passes God's love on to another person. Raymond does not possess or own his theophany solely for himself. The good word he received from God is meant to be shared and benefit others.

Basil wants to know how Raymond was able to get his family to accept his homosexual lifestyle. Raymond tells Basil that being homosexual is not a lifestyle, but his life. Homosexuality is not something he does, but who he is. Raymond also tells Basil that talking to his family was not easy and that he still hasn't spoken to his brother about it. But this is enough for Basil.

Black fathers always have trouble accepting their homosexual sons, Raymond tells Basil. "It's never easy for fathers. Especially Black fathers. They always think it's their fault."[19] When Raymond asks Basil if he is ready to claim his homosexuality and come out in the open, Basil responds that he is not thinking of that. Rather, he tells Raymond that he has some things to talk over with his father that won't be easy to say or easy for his father to hear. Raymond encourages Basil and assures him that things only become simpler when the truth is told. When Basil confides that he admires Raymond's happiness, Raymond responds with a theological affirmation that his happiness comes from God's grace.

Basil sits down and writes a letter to his father about the tragic night that his uncle molested him, but he doesn't send it. He tries to cry, but can't do that either. He just can't tell his father for fear of what it might do to his father. The book ends with Basil writing Raymond about that night instead.

In a subsequent book, *Not a Day Goes By*, Basil is still haunted by the night of his molestation. But the reader sees a more mature Basil. Basil is now the favorite uncle, but he is not condemned to repeat the past. Basil never even thinks about molesting his nephew.

Pastoral Theological Commentary

The Hampton group, psychotherapy, a close-knit family, and personal friendships are important examples of crucibles for privileging conversation with God. They are safe places where people can explore deep hurts as well as the grace of God. According to Harris's implied theologian, grace has a rippling effect. From the angel Kyle to Raymond to Basil to Basil's nephew, grace is contagious.

The implied psychotherapist is also crucial in Harris's novels. The bondage that one endured in the past does not have to remain. There is liberation available through talk therapy. But to be effective, therapy needs a mentor who exhibits care and who has the necessary experience to provide the kind of empathy that aids the care seeker to anticipate the future. Raymond is an example of a mentor who, by experiencing reconciliation with his own family, can give Basil guidance toward finding reconciliation with others. Revisiting the past with a caring other or with caring others can have liberating dimensions.

Conclusion

Throughout this book Job also serves as a model for conversation with God in the midst of tragedy and suffering. In Job 14:14 we find these words, "If mortals die, will they live again? All the days of my service I would wait, until my release should come." According to J. Gerald Janzen in his commentary of Job, this verse anticipates the development of a later Hebrew apocalyptic cosmic vision that gives Job hope in the midst of the deepest darkness in his life.[20] Janzen sees in this verse a hint that in the thinking of the Jewish people at this time, the world was divided into two ages—the present and the future with an in-between time. Thus, the possibility for redemption is always a hope for the future. In saying he will wait until his release, Job is saying that he anticipates a time that an encounter with God will bring resurrection and redemption.

In Harris's novels, especially the three named in this chapter, there is an anticipation of hope for Basil built on the experience that Raymond had with his family and with God. The grace of God permeates everything Raymond does after his encounter with the angel. In other words, Raymond's vision gave him a new identity and hope not only for himself but also for others.

In the story Basil asks, Why now? Why did he have to be visited by his past nightmares? Basil asks this question as do most people when they are in the throes of misfortune. The answer is *kairos*—God's time. God always takes the initiative in conversation when the time is right. Our task is to be like Raymond and receive it.

Grace and our sense of who we really are, our identity and our sexuality, are gifts from God. Our sense of who we are is forged in relationship to God through conversation, not just directly with God but also with friends, family, and caring professionals. Whether through the empathy offered through pastoral counseling or caring friends and family, God is present offering God's grace. And God can be counted on especially during difficult and tragic times.

Notes

1. Edward P. Wimberly, *Counseling African American Marriages and Families* (Louisville: Westminster John Knox, 1997), 29-32.

2. Sylvia Ann Hewlett and Cornel West, *The Way Against Parents: What We Can Do for American's Beleaguered Moms and Dads* (New York: Houghton Mifflin: 1998), 30.

3. Richard B. Hays, "The Biblical Witness Concerning Homosexuality," *Staying the Course: Supporting the Church's Position on Homosexuality*, Maxie D. Dunnam and H. Newton Malony, eds. (Nashville: Abingdon Press, 2003), 74.

4. Ibid., 8.

5. E. Lynn Harris, *Abide With Me* (New York: Anchor Books, 2000); and *Just As I Am: A Novel* (New York: Doubleday, 1994).

6. This view about sexual identity formation embraces the notion that identity formation is grounded in God and not in our sexuality. See Richard Hays, *The Moral Vision of the New Testament, Community, Cross, New Creation: A Contemporary Introduction to New Testament Ethics* (Harper San Francisco, 1996), 396-80; 391.

7. Richard Hays, *The Moral Vision of the New Testament*, 379.

8. Harris, *Abide With Me*, 346.

9. The implied author is not the actual author. Rather, the implied author is the author that appears as the book unfolds and whose intention may not be the same as the real author. The implied author is the rhetorical device through which the story is told. See Mark Allan Powell, *What Is Narrative Criticism?* (Minneapolis: Fortress Press, 1980), 27.

10. Edward P. Wimberly, *Pastoral Counseling and Spiritual Values: A Black Point of View* (Nashville: Abingdon Press, 1982), 63-69.

11. Harris, *Abide With Me*, 348.

12. Ibid., 349.

13. Ibid., 350.

14. See note 5 above.

15. E. Lynn Harris, *Just As I Am*, 368.

16. E. Lynn Harris, *If This World Were Mine* (New York: Doubleday, 1997).

17. Ibid., 290.

18. Ibid.

19. Ibid., 310.

20. J. Gerald Janzen, *Job, Interpretation: A Bible Commentary for Teaching and Preaching* (Atlanta: John Knox Press, 1985), 110-13.

CHAPTER FOUR

BECOMING HOLY

A s discussed in chapter 3, E. Lynn Harris puts forth two theological points in his novels. The first has to do with the important role of the mentor: the character of Raymond as he mediates the love of God. Mentoring others can be a dimension of holiness as one lives out the implications of God's grace. The second is that the energy manifested through God's grace does not dissipate but only multiplies as it is passed from person to person. After Raymond receives God's message from the angel Kyle, he passes the grace he received on to Basil who in turn passes it on to his nephew. From this we see that those who encounter the grace of God do not receive it only for their own well-being but also for the benefit of others. Grace is not a gift for the lone individual; it is a gift from God freely given to all and meant to be shared through acts of grace toward others.

In the Wesleyan tradition, holiness focuses on conversations related to the perfection of the love of God in us. For our purposes, the perfection of love is about privileging conversations that emerge from the example of Jesus' sacrificial love. These conversations surrounding the perfection of God's love assume that one has already been restored to a right relationship with God and is living out the Christian story. Once one accepts God's prevenient grace and is justified, or put in right relationship with God, one can then grow in holiness or sanctification toward the example of Jesus' sacrificial love. This means we grow in the direction of God's intent for our lives—to be like Jesus. Said another way, the more we learn to privilege conversation with God, the more clearly we hear God's voice and the better we can distinguish God's voice from the competing voices of the world. Said yet another way, it is as though at first we see in a mirror dimly (1 Corinthians 13:12) but then we see face-to-face. Our face comes to reflect the face of God. Our holiness comes to reflect Jesus' love for God, self, and others.

Holiness is the direction sanctifying grace takes us. In this chapter I want to explore conversations about holiness that appear in the novels I have already introduced as well as in another. Sanctification comes as the result of living out one's own call in relationship to God's unfolding drama of salvation, which includes the redemption of the entire world. Sanctifying conversation refers to privileging the talk that leads one to imitate the love of Jesus.

Approaches to Holiness

Reflection on chapters 1-3 will help reveal the nature of sanctification implicit in conversations about identity formation, healing, and transformation. For example, the life of Jefferson in Ernest Gaines's *A Lesson Before Dying* shows us something important about sanctification. Jefferson learned to privilege the conversations he heard about the death of Jesus on the cross such that he sought to pattern his life and death based on Jesus' example. Jefferson became a powerful witness to those who surrounded him at his death. The peace on Jefferson's face spoke of the love in his heart for his friends and executioners.

Clifford Harris's implicit view of sanctification can be seen in his autobiography, *Death Dance*. This book is about Clifford's reconnection with his family. In this account of his transformation we learn that Clifford keeps a book about the life of Jesus on his nightstand. The book, *The Desire of Ages*, lays unopened nearby; but as he begins to reminisce, the vivid word pictures of Jesus that his parents painted return to his memory.[1]

For Clifford, the process of being restored to a right relationship with God begins with the grace that keeps him alive despite his death wish. After the providential rediscovery of the book about Jesus, this same grace begins to cleanse him from within and eventually leads him to forgive himself. He says that he can stand today and do what God calls him to do because he knows that he is forgiven despite all the pain that he caused in the lives of others.

After a dramatic transformation, Clifford enters into the process of sanctification. Slowly he begins to take part in the life of the church, and so his place within God's story continues to take shape. As Clifford participates in the Seventh-day Adventist Church, the church's convictions about personal piety begin to take hold in his life. He describes discovering his purpose in life as he participates in a Twelve Step program.[2] As one might expect, Clifford's transformation is couched in language that reflects both the personal piety of Seventh-day Adventists and the Twelve Step program. By combining the two languages, he is able to put together a meaningful conversation that now ministers to many other persons who are recovering from substance abuse.

The implicit theology in E. Lynn Harris's work makes it clear that God's grace, whether prevenient, justifying, or sanctifying, is open to all persons. One can receive the fullness of God's grace irrespective of one's sexual orientation. Self-avowed, practicing homosexuals can participate in selfless, self-sacrificing love in the care of others. What counts for Harris is that one puts one's relationship with God over all other relationships.

In the theology in which I was raised and which informs me today, God's grace embraces everyone regardless of sexual practices. In my theology, each person must work out his or her theology with God, and no one has a right to interfere in another's personal walk with God. This does not mean, however, that people cannot enter into conversation with each other to better inform or nurture, but it does mean that in the end each person is responsible for his or her relationship with God.

God offers a personal relationship, fellowship, and conversation to all regardless of sexual orientation. This point of view trusts God and the person to work out his or her own salvation. This entering into a conversation with others about their behavior and their relationship with God is by invitation only. The sacredness of a person's personal relationship with God should be upheld at all costs.

The book of Job provides us with a challenging view of sanctification. Job's life teaches us that the process of becoming holy must take place in the midst of one's own suffering. In the midst of suffering, God encounters us and provides sustaining fellowship. But sometimes persons are so wounded that they cannot bear to encounter anyone or anything else.

Often when a person makes a decision to seek counseling, that decision is a decisive act that begins the healing process. Normally wounded persons defend themselves against the prospect of further hurt. They cover or disguise their hurt in an effort just to get by or to stop feeling the pain inside. Entering the counseling process is like the client offering a tentative invitation. It is then the job of the counselor to expose the wound so it can be shared and thus eventually healed. This task is a delicate operation and not something to be entered into without sufficient reflection, training, and supervision. Often pastoral counselors make a way for God. Through empathic listening and informed feedback, the counselor can guide the client to a place where he or she can open up to God and begin to engage God in conversation. The very fact that a person can sustain fellowship with God or anyone else is a sign of growing health. The more a person can engage in sustained fellowship with God, the more he or she can participate in God's redemptive activity in the world in a realistic way.

Uncomfortable as it might make us feel, Job teaches us that suffering is a sure sign of God's redeeming of creation. This view is predicated on a theology of redemptive suffering where God's work of redemption takes place in the midst of chaos, conflict, and evil. Conversation with God, then, does not negate the possibility of personal suffering; but the chaos, conflict, and evil with which we live as human beings necessitate the fellowship of God. Making conversation with God primary enables us to endure and ultimately to find salvation even if sanctification comes to fruition after death.

Thus the book of Job is for some about the learning that comes as one participates in the redemptive activity of God taking place at the cosmic level.[3] As Job struggles with conversations he has with his friends, he revises his notion that holiness means the absence of suffering. The book of Job, rather, sets the stage for the later theological belief that holiness must become a reality in the midst of suffering. Suffering does not mean that one has been abandoned by God or that one has sinned, but it means that one has entered into God's process of redemption. Suffering is the necessary circumstance that one must confront as the result of accepting one's vocation in God's redemptive work. Our suffering means that we have entered into God's story at the deepest possible level. Thus suffering is a sure sign of God's presence rather than absence. As we suffer, we imitate Christ and thus we are sanctified in the eyes of God.[4]

What Looks Like Crazy on an Ordinary Day

Pearl Cleage's novel, *What Looks Like Crazy on an Ordinary Day*, is about a person who, after having contracted HIV, returns home to find genuine love and an affirming community. The plot of the book is driven by central questions that are both secular and religious. The basic question is not who gave the chief protagonist HIV, rather what will the protagonist do with this disease when it suddenly becomes a part of life. Secularly, the question is a practical one, How does one survive on a daily basis with HIV? Religiously, the question is, How does one make a meaningful life despite living with a potentially life-threatening reality?

In the novel there is tension between the traditional functioning of a local church congregation and the formation of a para-church that provides fellowship and nurture despite the local congregation. The formal institutional church is painted as one concerned with the appearance of social respectability while the other is primarily concerned with the spiritual nurturing of others in the faith.

The novel also raises the existential questions, How does one return home to remake one's life after messing it up? Does nostalgia ever get a person anywhere? and, How does one best live in the face of death?

From a holiness perspective, the novel contrasts the life of self-indulgence and running from commitment with a life of embracing service to others with commitment. The implicit notion of holiness in this book is that of having the courage to face the consequences of one's past sins while at the same time embracing the significant opportunities that life has to bring. For example, although the chief protagonist, Ava, laments the fact that she contracted HIV from sleeping with someone she didn't even care about, she nevertheless has to face the consequences of her choice. But by facing her past in conversation with those who are spiritually nurturing, she finds hope to make the most of her life despite having it dramatically disrupted.

The Nature of Retribution

In the sections below I will discuss some of the relevant themes of Cleage's implied theology. The first theme is the nature of retribution or punishment for sins. Early in the novel the question of *natural retribution* is raised without apology. Here *natural* refers to natural theology that postulates that it is possible to derive knowledge of the created order without reference to divine revelation or to God.[5] The implied theology of the novel raises the question of whether one must pay with one's life for having promiscuous sex without love or any commitment.[6] In fact, the protagonist says that what makes her crazy is the thought that she is paying with her life for having sex without love. While *crazy* refers to reflection on the past without hope for the future, the book is really about the courage it takes for Ava to face the future and embrace the real opportunities for hope she actually has in the present.

Several years ago, early in the conversations about HIV and AIDS in this country, it was politically incorrect to raise questions about retribution. Persons who did, however, go ahead and raise this issue were thought to be insensitive and overly judgmental. This novel is helpful in this regard because the issue is raised and disposed of rather quickly by the implied theologian. The author's implied theology focuses instead on the process of redemption.

As in the case with the book of Job, the question of retributive justice never gets resolved in the novel. Whether retribution for sin is part of the created order does not receive a lot of attention. What Job and this novel seem to be about is pointing to the creative possibilities and opportunities for hope despite the presence of suffering. Whatever the cause of suffering, whether one's own actions or the actions of others, the truth is that suffering does not have to be the last word. Meaning and a full life are possible.

The implied theology of this book can suggest to the pastoral counselor that it is possible to pursue God conversation without using explicit theological language. It is possible to employ natural categories of human possibility despite the existence of suffering. Within the created order itself, there will always be opportunities to fulfill one's life despite the past because novelty and possibility are part of creation.[7] The implication is that the pastoral counselor can facilitate meaning and hope by reference to the natural opportunities for novelty that are part of creation. One does not have to be overcome with guilt over past decisions or the futility of living. One can move forward in hope despite being diagnosed with HIV. For example, I think of the special life of the former NBA basketball star, Magic Johnson. His life took on sudden significance when he discovered that he had contracted the HIV virus. His personal lifestyle was transformed, and he began a process of service to the community that is rivaled by very few. In addition, spirituality played a very significant role in his new lease on life.

In explicit theological language, it is the grace of God that undergirds the creative possibilities that are part of the created order. Moreover, redemption and forgiveness of sin are possible because of the presence of grace. In addition, as Cleage's book suggests, moving toward holiness is also possible through caring for oneself and others.

The Nature of Redemption

The implied theologian in the novel presents redemption through several distinctions. These distinctions include having sex versus making love, work versus vocation, celibacy versus promiscuity, and a committed relationship versus a casual relationship. The novel also connects commitment in relationships and real love as opposed to just having sex. Ava's mother committed suicide apparently as the result of the pain of being in an intimate relationship with Ava's father. Ava visualized the cost involved in commitment and decided casual living would be her way of preventing the suffering her mother bore.[8]

As we witness Ava's transformation, we also see how real love or true love becomes a goal. As love becomes her goal, sex is put back into its proper relational context. Sex becomes an aspect of a loving relationship. It is a means of a loving relationship and not the goal. As her fear decreases and her ability to enter into a committed relationship grows, her propensity to commit increases.

The issue of celibacy also surfaces in the novel.[9] In Ava's process of transformation there is a period of abstinence when sexual activity is put on hold. For the protagonist, sex had been an escape from really encountering others; sex was a substitute for a real relationship. The implied theologian in the novel helps the reader to see that sex can be disconnected from genuine care and intimacy and become only a physical act for some. Theologically, sex is much more than a physical act alone; rather it is an expression of a genuine relationship. Its purpose is to communicate and strengthen a relationship that already exists. Celibacy, then, is necessary so that she can enter into a real and committed relationship. It is only when our heroine seeks genuine intimacy that true love can emerge.

Celibacy is also portrayed as being essential for the process of healing, particularly when sex has served as an escape from genuine encounter with another. The sexual act is a form of intimate bonding even if there is no other aspect of relationship present. Just like when you try to separate two pieces of paper that have been glued together, and the papers tear, when two people separate after being glued together by sex, there is wounding for both. The wound eventually scars over, but these scars make it harder to bond with someone else the next time. In extreme cases with multiple sex partners, a person can become so scarred that bonding with anyone is impossible. Hence celibacy is necessary to give persons a chance to heal.

I remember one of my counselees saying that in sex we internalize each person with whom we sleep, and getting those persons out of our inner lives is a complicated process. She said, celibacy was a must because she had multiple partners. Healing and transformation for her was a process of exorcism of internalized personalities that required a period of celibacy. She said this process of exorcising was so difficult that one would hardly ever desire to reenter a casual sexual relationship again.

A significant dimension of the transformation process for the protagonist, Ava, is the discovery of her vocation, by which I mean the dimension of service in her work. She begins to use her job as a hairdresser to affirm others. As she grows in her understanding of her profession, she comes to realize how she can minister to others. Even the simple act of washing another's hair becomes a means by which she serves others.

At first Ava thinks all there is to fixing hair is vain emptiness and looking good for others. As she listens more carefully while the women talk, she begins to realize that their coming to her is symbolic of something far deeper. She then discovers that only half the time the issue is looking good for the brothers; the other half it is about community building. For the implied theologian, community building is about having a safe and secure place to talk without being censored, to be affirmed without having to pretend to be someone else, and finally not to have to worry about exchanging sex for being cared for. Cleage suggests that community building is valuable, so valuable that women will pay between thirty and fifty dollars twice a week for it.[10]

As the plot develops Ava begins to see her role as ensuring that a caring environment and community exist. Providing active listening, affirmation, and selfless love become her passion and her commitment. This becomes her vocation; she finds meaning in giving herself to others.

Caring for others while fixing hair is not the only way Ava learns to care for others. She also volunteers to help her sister care for a group of teenage single pregnant girls. As she assists these girls, her concern is to make sure the church is relevant in their lives. This church, which is also her church home, preaches hellfire and damnation. While she does not agree with the theology, she tries to tolerate it as best she can; but it just doesn't seem to be very realistic about the real needs of the community, particularly of these teenagers.

The mentoring in the church becomes problematic when Ava and her sister, Joyce, decide to demonstrate to the girls how to use a condom. Their concern is to help the girls avoid becoming pregnant again. They figure that the girls are already sexually active and therefore need realistic help with prevention. The condom demonstration, however, sadly leads to the church expelling the mentoring group. Some church people think demonstrating how to use a condom sends the wrong message—a message of permission to have sex. Some feel that the demonstration means that the church is sanctioning sex outside of marriage. One person even feels that the demonstration desecrates the church.[11]

Even though the mentoring group is expelled from the church, this does not weaken Ava's or Joyce's commitment to those girls. Before long they find an alternative place to meet. And they continue their efforts of following their vision to make a difference.

Reconnecting with Home

Another theme is the significance of home and the importance of reconnecting with it for transformation. The novel shows that small-town life has the same kinds of problems that city life has, particularly in regard to drugs, HIV, and AIDS. In an effort to increase their turf and make more money, gangs from the city target small towns. Small towns may have smaller police forces, and they may also have deep pockets. From the gangs' point of view, there is a lot of money to be made and not much business competition. One of the characters even says that small-town life doesn't save or redeem people like it once did.[12] Nevertheless, Ava comes back to her small hometown for just that—salvation and redemption. By returning home, she learns to reconnect with her family and finally with her true self.

As in most love stories, girl meets boy; in this book Ava meets Eddie. Eddie found that by returning home the small-town life enabled him to slow down and implement the lessons that he had learned. He had served in Vietnam and had been haunted by its memories. Reconnecting with home allowed him to take his reflections on his Vietnam experience and put them into practice.[13] He felt the city life would have made him for-get the wisdom he had accumulated.

The key lesson Eddie learns is that when you are dealing with major issues in life, home is the best place to be. He draws an analogy from the tunnels that the Vietcong dug and how they stocked them with supplies, knowing that they were in the war for the long haul. The same can be said of facing the serious issues of personal transformation and the drive for holiness—home is where the long-term resources are. Home is the best place to be because it makes you stronger.

Generativity

The final theme I will explore from Cleage's novel is generativity. Generativity refers to mentoring the next generation through the wisdom that elders pass on. Cleage is concerned that black girls are mentored so that they can have safe sex. This concern recognizes the fact that sexual involvement is a reality among teens and that protection against preg-nancy and disease is very important. While the author is concerned about this, her implied theology communicates an additional message. This message has to do with the issue of settling. *Settling* is a term used to describe black women accepting less in terms of their ideal mate when more is possible.[14]

When the teen group is kicked out of the church for having a condom demonstration, the group has to become more formal and organized for survival. So they develop a mission statement. This mission statement and its derivative goals focus on nurturing free, independent, responsible women who can care for themselves, raise their children correctly, and choose lovers wisely.[15] The project of developing black womanhood includes training in home economics, self-defense, sex education and midwifery, childhood development, literacy, health and recreation, home repair, and spiritual practice.

The issue of settling surfaces in regard to sex education. The two sis-ters, Ava and Joyce, discuss the merits of having sex without love. The focus is not on waiting to have sex before marriage, but on whether one should have sex with someone one does not like. The concern is whether one should wait to have sex until one finds a mate one really cares about. While Ava feels that love is rare and therefore not a likely standard for having sex, Joyce feels that it is worth the wait. Joyce feels that one could wait indefinitely for sex in order to wait for love first.

The point is that sex education should involve options that take seriously the rare as well as the common. Abstinence and waiting for love are realistic, but safe sex is the best option to be taken by those who feel they have to settle for sex without love.

Pastoral Theological Reflection

In this section I will explore various themes in relationship as expressed in Cleage's novel to see what can be learned about sanctification. Pastoral theological reflection takes many forms. Here I will focus on that dimension of pastoral theological reflection that helps us enter the implicit theology of sanctification from a doctrinal theological point of view. The key concern is with the level of God conversation that can be privileged.

This novel makes a very clear distinction between conversations that are spiritual in nature and those that center on religious respectability. This novel portrays general religious life from a secular perspective as being preoccupied with social acceptability rather than with meeting the true needs of human beings. Therefore, spirituality is conceived of as genuine concern for the growth and development of persons holistically.

Personal piety is also a concern. In the novel, transformation and the recognition of unhealthy living go hand in hand. In this view transformation and sanctification come from general lessons that women develop for themselves as they live and learn from their mistakes. Cleage comes from a religious background; she grew up in the home of a minister. The religious background in her novel was subtle, but it was the source of norms that were revealed by the implied theologian. Thus, one can safely say that the ability of her characters to learn from mistakes included the skill of drawing on tradition for its wisdom. The novel, however, sees the knowledge that comes from traditional sources as inadequate. The church leadership is viewed as having a completely different agenda from offering genuine love and care for others. It appears that the church leadership is made up of people too broken and too wrapped up in their own problems to really reach out and care for others. The novel reveals that the congregational leaders are often the walking wounded who leave human casualties behind rather than help heal others.

My own assessment is that this book has a well thought out implied theology of sanctification that includes an understanding of how grace and love can be transmitted from one generation to the next. The narrative faith story that undergirds most theologies is missing, but the core message of love of self and love of others echoes New Testament concerns.

The most significant pastoral theological issue is the role of love in sexual relationships. The ideal of finding true love so that sex and true love are related is central to the book. The protagonist waits for nearly half of her life before she finds true love. The ideal for romantic true love has dominated the black church's view of sexuality and its practice. This is to say that there have been at least two conversations. The first is the ideal of finding true love and waiting until marriage before having sex. The second is a conversation that true love is rare; therefore, one must settle for sex without love to have at least some satisfaction in life. One paints an overly rosy picture of intimate relationships, but the other paints an overly pessimistic one. Putting these two together we end up with the notion that some will find true love, rare though it is; but others will have to settle. The book seems to say that only the lucky find true love and are able to live out the ideal image of sex within marriage. In Cleage's latest novel, *I Wish I Had a Red Dress*,[16] she takes up the notion that the wait for true love pays dividends. Joyce, the sister who remains celibate following the death of her husband, meets the love of her life after many long years. Thus, her patience is rewarded. The significance of this is that celibacy is a conversation that is becoming more prominent, given the fact that we are discovering that the risk of sexually transmitted diseases rules out casual sex altogether.

Responsible Grace

This novel *What Looks Like Crazy on an Ordinary Day* describes what Randy L. Maddox calls "responsible grace."[17] Responsible grace refers to the fact that God's grace will not save us without our own grace-empowered, but unforced, participation.[18] The goal of such *response-able* grace from a narrative point of view is to enable the empowerment of self and others toward a *responsible* participation in God's unfolding drama of salvation. The author and implied theologian of the novel focus on how those on the periphery of the church may embody the grace necessary to move people to responsible growth and living.

Several dimensions of responsible grace are disclosed in the novel. The first is that one can encounter grace in the midst of living. In the novel, grace is encountered in the process of reconnecting with others from the past as well as in recalling one's early formative roots. It is a process of remembering that connects the heroine with her original meaning-making environment. Despite all of the weaknesses of the church leadership, the church is viewed with some positive dynamics that lead some to selfless service.

The second dimension is learning to accept and be transformed by the grace that is offered. In the novel we see how Ava finds the love she seeks when she returns home. Here at home she receives her sister's love and then the love of a man. Such genuine love appears to be a gift which is undeserved and which comes as a real surprise. The implied theologian pictures grace as an unlimited reservoir of love that is available to all.

The third dimension of responsible grace involves enabling Ava to be a better listener and minister. Her hairdressing business becomes her ministry to others. Ava responds to grace as a natural outgrowth of the grace she receives. This is a core message of the book.

From the perspective of Job, this novel is not about redemptive suffering. Redemptive suffering comes when one who lives righteously suffers hardship anyhow, but *What Looks Like Crazy on an Ordinary Day* is about the remedial suffering that comes as a result of our sins and shortcomings. Redemptive suffering is that suffering that comes because we have sided with God, and as a result we have gotten caught in a cosmic struggle. In the cosmic struggle we participate with God as God overcomes evil. We become the enemies of Satan as a result. Remedial suffering comes when we actually violate a strong value, and we need corrective experience in order to learn. Here a strong value in the case of Ava is not settling for sex without genuine intimacy. Through his struggle and God conversation, Job learns to distinguish between the two types of suffering.

This chapter reflected on the meaning of holiness that surfaced in several novels. Undergirding this discussion was the Wesleyan notion of sanctification or the process of becoming a whole person empowered by grace. One conclusion is that it is possible to talk about grace as a source of power for transformation that is part of the natural order of things as well as to talk about grace confessionally as part of a faith tradition. In either case transforming grace is a reality in life.

Notes

1. Clifford Harris, *Death Dance: A True Story of Drug Addiction and Redemption* (Grand Terrance, Calif.: Drug Alternative Program, 1999), 232.

2. Ibid., 253-65.

3. J. Gerald Janzen, *Job, Interpretation: A Bible Commentary for Teaching and Preaching* (Atlanta: John Knox Press, 1985), 121.

4. Alan Richardson and John Bowden, *The Westminster Dictionary of Christian Theology* (Philadelphia: Westminster Press, 1983), 555-56.

5. Ibid., 393.

6. Pearl Cleage, *What Looks Like Crazy on an Ordinary Day* (New York: Anchor Books, 1997), 7-8.

7. For a discussion of how guilt and possibility are part of the created order, see Thomas Oden, *The Structure of Awareness* (Nashville: Abingdon Press, 1969), 83-84.

8. Cleage, *What Looks Like Crazy,* 48.

9. Ibid. 34.

10. Ibid., 81-82.

11. Ibid., 92-96.

12. Ibid., 24.

13. Ibid., 118-20.

14. Edward P. Wimberly, *Recalling Our Own Stories: Spiritual Renewal of Religious Caregivers* (San Francisco: Jossey-Bass, 1997), 39-41.

15. Cleage, *What Looks Like Crazy,* 157-60.

16. Pearl Cleage, *I Wish I Had a Red Dress* (New York: Harper Collins, 2001).

17. Randy L. Maddox, *Responsible Grace: John Wesley's Practical Theology* (Nashville: Kingswood Books, 1994), 19.

18. Ibid.

CHAPTER FIVE

RESPONSIBLE GRACE

Partners with God in Redemption

The major focus of this chapter is how privileging conversation with God can facilitate healing for those who have been set apart by God for ordained ministry. To examine the critical concerns for those God has called and anointed for ordained ministry and their need for emotional, interpersonal, and spiritual healing, I will look at three novels. The first is Ernest Gaines's novel entitled *In My Father's House*; the second is *What Looks Like Crazy on an Ordinary Day* by Pearl Cleage; and the third is *Men of Brewster Place* by Gloria Naylor. All three novels raise significant questions about whether God's elect can be healed so that they can be positive forces in helping others. These novels portray clergy as walking wounded who are caught in the miry clay of personal problems that inflict wounds on others—as people who make problems rather than find solutions to problems.

Each novel depicts the ordained clergy as victims trapped in much the same way as everybody else. It appears that the God they proclaim has no power or impact on their lives. They are caught up in conversations that make them impotent and irrelevant. This chapter will explore how, despite their obvious human flaws, to help clergy become responsible healers.

How do hurting ministers become whole persons so that they can be responsible partners with God in the redemption of the world? Job's pattern of privileging conversation with God can again help us answer this question. Toward the beginning of the book of Job, we see Job suffer staggering losses—his property, his family, his health. We see Job suffer until it seems that there is nothing left. Even the words his friends offer only bring more suffering. Then in a great act of courage, Job looks at his suffering. Even in the midst of his suffering, Job has the wherewithal to look his suffering in the face. This means that he still has the strength to pull away from his suffering enough to reflect on it. Another way to think about this is to say that he uses the intrapsychic defense of intellectualization as a beginning point in a search to find meaning and therefore hope for his life.

Job begins with the conventional wisdom of his day to understand what is happening to him. His three consoling friends help him in this process by helping Job sift through the tradition. Ultimately, however, he finds the conventional wisdom lacking. His suffering just does not fit and his religious tradition is inadequate for his present experience. Something has to change.

Job is described as a good person, a religious person, perhaps much like the persons who are called into ministry. In Job's day, a good person observed the totality of the law. In our day, ministers are expected to be good people who practice what they preach. Ministers are expected to be outwardly religious; but more than that, ministers are often expected to be inwardly pious if not holy. In an ideal sense they are expected, at the very least, to be on the road to perfection, to borrow a Methodist concept. At ordination United Methodist clergy are asked if they expect to be made perfect in love in this life. The answer given is, "Yes." Needless to say, many people demand a degree of perfection from their pastors while at the same time knowing this is impossible. Indeed, some pastors have the same difficult expectations for themselves. Obviously the conventional wisdom about what it means to be a pastor is tinged with unrealistic expectations. Both meeting and not meeting these expectations can be painful. I once knew a young divinity student who had such high expectations of himself and his academic achievement that when he failed to do as well as he thought he should, he committed suicide. While this scenario is not unique to divinity students, it does point out the tyranny of unrealistic expectations and the suffering they can cause. Like Job, one has to find a way to look at one's suffering, reflect upon it, and move on. The book of Job would also suggest that moving on also means finding God and new meaning.

Michael White's concept of membership can help us understand the process of emergent meaning. Membership, according to White, refers to those original-meaning contexts where the first conversations about the meaning of life took place. In the case of perfection, the focus will be on those original conversations and relational contexts where the notions of clergy perfection were learned. The key to transforming the meaning of perfection is to return to those original contexts and revisit those original meanings much in the same way that Job did. Then, and only then, can the revisiting foster new understandings as one struggles to find God.

In My Father's House

There is a well-known saying that the preacher can help everybody except members of his or her own family. Why is this? Why is it so hard for preachers to care for their own? Is it because the work of God is so consuming that we must sacrifice our families? Is it because the work of caring for others takes precedence over all other things including our families? Or is it because the work of caring for our families is very difficult; and, therefore, we as ministers are completely unprepared to tend to the work of ministry and care for our families simultaneously?

In the novel, *In My Father's House*, Ernest Gaines explores in depth one preacher's problems in caring for his families. Gaines explores the ramifications of pastors who cannot manage their home life. The book begins when a successful civil rights worker and pastor in a small southern town is suddenly visited by his son. This son is the fruit of a previous relationship. The father, Rev. Phillip Martin, has not seen his son for more than twenty years and faints from shock when he recognizes his son, Robert. Phillip realizes that his past has caught up with him. All the old memories are overwhelming and disturbing, as are his feelings of guilt and remorse.

Phillip knows he must attend to his son even at the expense of his civil rights work. He seeks to get to know his son and to learn about the world he left far behind. While Phillip wants to reconcile with his past and his son, his son has another agenda. When Robert was a little boy, Phillip abandoned the family. Robert suffered with the feeling that he had to carry the load of his mother, brothers, and sisters. The family fell on hard times, and then a tragic accident occurred. Robert felt it was his fault, and the pain of grief and guilt drove him to mental illness. When he hears about his father's new identity and successful life, Robert is angry. He comes into Phillip's life for only one thing—revenge. He decides to commit suicide.

As Phillip is engaged in his daily devotion one morning, he reads Psalm 102. This is a supplication for God not to hide God's face and to hear his voice. He knows he is in deep and uncharted waters and he needs God's guiding hand to navigate the turbulent waters. He realizes that he neglected the family he created in his irresponsible youth, and he suffers. Phillip's suffering is corrective; it is something from which he can learn.

Phillip resolves to get to know his son even if it means neglecting his ministry and his new family. But his son will not be known. In an act of sacrifice, Phillip returns to the old community to find out for himself what had happened. While he is there, Phillip receives word that his son has committed suicide. The novel ends with Phillip, completely distraught, with no earthly idea of what to do. His new life as a moral leader is cracked. Nothing he has learned, no wisdom he has gained prepared him for this. Now the real suffering begins.

Doubtless, Phillip Martin was guilty of past sins. But because he confessed them, he also thought he had been forgiven and that his sins were over and done with. He was dumbfounded when his past fiercely resurfaced to derail him. In desperation he asked God, "Why Father? Why? I think I have served you well; I've served my people well. Why?"[1]

We can draw several key conversation themes from Phillip's supplication. The first theme is God's punishment for past sins, or divine retribution. The second is doing penance for one's sins. The third is confronting the destructive consequences of one's sins even when one feels forgiven. This third theme is especially important because it relates to one's spiritual growth. Past sins surface when corrective learning is needed to move the sinner to the next stage of growth and development in his or her relationship with God. The resurfacing of sins is often a clue for the sinner, even the forgiven sinner, to revise his or her life in order to move into deeper partnership in God's salvation drama. It is a call to responsible grace.

Responsible grace reflects John Wesley's view that God's grace is not static, but it requires us to go beyond and attain new goals.[2] Gaines's book illustrates the continual need for fresh infusions of God's grace. When Phillip Martin confronted his past, he may have needed God's grace to ensure his forgiveness, but he moved ahead largely on his own power. When he was confronted with his son's suicide and his present situation fell apart, he found himself distraught and alone. Where was God then? What will Phillip do? Does he have enough of a relationship with God to grieve, learn, and move on? Gaines leaves us with no answers.

According to Phillip's conventional wisdom, his sins would eventually be found out. His thinking was that he had done all the right things—face his past, confess his sins, receive forgiveness, and turn his life completely around—yet he was still being punished; and much worse, his son was suffering as well. What more did Phillip need to do? After all, for fifteen years he had been the epitome of Christian character and service. He had done his part; why wasn't God doing God's?

Phillip needed God in a new way. He needed a fresh infusion of God's grace. Like Job, he turns to God for understanding. But as he searches, he only finds himself experiencing more and more pain. When the pain becomes unbearable, he even thinks about running away and escaping through wine, women, and song as in former times. He is helpless and hopeless. Where is God now for this man of God? Ernest Gaines leaves the reader hungry for an answer. We are hungry for an answer just as Phillip is hungry, just as his son hungered. Perhaps Gaines is saying that hunger, even spiritual hunger, can be the first step toward being filled—filled with God's grace. But it doesn't have to lead to being filled at all; sometimes people are just destroyed instead.

From our comfortable position on the outside, we can say that Phillip needed inner healing; we can even say this rather glibly. And he does, but Gaines draws us into Phillip's dilemma, confusion, and bewilderment until we recognize that sometimes people can get lost in their own pain and suffering. What does it take to have the stamina to keep seeking? Is there ever a place where one is too lost for God to find them? I think I will leave you with that question.

According to Wesleyan theology, transformation is a lifelong process, which is fueled by God's sanctifying grace, the grace that will not let us go. Past sins may resurface to teach us new lessons, but they can also be reservoirs of new growth potential. Past sins are old wounds that need inner healing, but these old wounds can also become sources of renewed strength. Ernest Gaines, at least in this book, does not present this hopeful perspective; rather, he seems to suggest that clergy are especially prone to broken relationships. Not only is Gaines not aware of this inner healing possibility for clergy, other African American novelists are not aware of this theology. In fact, Pearl Cleage and Gloria Naylor present clergy as the walking wounded who are actual detriments to others and to the community.

Novels by Gloria Naylor and Pearl Cleage

Novels by Gloria Naylor and Pearl Cleage assume the sin and retribution wisdom regarding the lives of clergy. In fact, they present clergy as imperfect human beings who are incapable of learning from past sins. These novels, in particular, portray clergy as victims of their own inner lives with few redeeming qualities.

As discussed in the previous chapter, Pearl Cleage's novel, *What Looks Like Crazy on an Ordinary Day*[3] is about a woman who contracts the HIV virus and how she eventually finds true love and vital vocation. Despite the heroine's acquiring the disease as a result of a promiscuous sexual relationship, she is able to learn from her experience and find grace in the midst of tragedy.

Ava Johnson, the heroine, carries out her new sense of vocation and mission by working with her sister to mentor young pregnant mothers. The setting for the mentoring is a church that dependably supports this ministry. All goes well until the pastor's wife sees Ava and her sister demonstrating the use of condoms. Horrified that the church might be perceived as promoting promiscuity, the pastor's wife sees to it that the program is expelled from the church. Not satisfied with ridding the church of these people, she threatens to have the program completely dismantled by trying to terminate the public funds that also support the program.

Just as the program is about to be totally derailed, we learn that the pastor's wife, Gerry Anderson, has a secret. Keeping this secret is her hidden agenda. Later it becomes apparent that the pastor had been removed from his previous congregation for sexually inappropriate behavior. Several teenage boys reported that he fondled them. The consequent investigation revealed compelling evidence against the pastor, and he was removed from the church, agreeing to leave town and get therapy.

The novel ends with Ava carving out places to fulfill her new vocation; the teen pregnancy program continues, although with uncertain funding. We don't learn much more about the pastor, but it remains obvious that he has not changed and that his wife is trying to shield him (and herself perhaps) from further disgrace and embarrassment. The obvious implication is that the pastor may have had some kind of inappropriate relationship with at least one of the youth. Cleage portrays the pastor with no redeeming qualities.

In the novel, *Men of Brewster Place*,[4] Gloria Naylor also portrays a clergyman with few redeeming qualities. The book is about black men who seem to have been victims of racism and hard times. She describes them as pitiful creatures who have been recruited into identities and stories not of their own making. Most of these characters are incapable of adequate functioning for a variety of reasons.

Two characters stand out. One is a promising young community organizer, Abshu. The other is the local preacher named the Right Reverend Moreland T. Woods. The young man has contempt for the Right Reverend because the pastor, as the first black on the city council, votes to destroy the rooming house known as Brewster Place. Apparently the pastor made a political deal with the white power structure to close down a solid symbol of stability for the black community in order to gain personal favor. In his very first act, the Right Reverend sells out the black community. Not only that, but Abshu gets the pastor removed from office because of inappropriate sexual activity with women of the community.

Naylor shows how angry the Right Reverend is with God. He is angry because he feels God has slighted him by not making him significant enough. Further, he feels that God, like the deacon board of his church, is holding him back. A skillful manipulator, Woods uses his church and deacon board to launch a political career. Woods blackmails some deacon board members into helping him run for city council. His goal is not community service but selfish gain, and it leads to his downfall. But important for our purposes is the fact that Naylor gives the Right Reverend few redeeming qualities.

Beyond the Perfectionist Conversation

Undergirding all three of these novels is an implicit theological conversation about perfection that, in the authors' eyes, should result from conversion. This contrasts to a notion of grace presented in this book that emphasizes the need to grow and develop beyond one's initial relationship with God. It is as if to say, according to these authors, that what happens following conversion is static; one has arrived, so to speak. Grace, on the other hand, is a dynamic quality that continues to flow through the lives of individuals and the church giving us hope and wisdom. Grace gives us the opportunity to deepen and broaden our relationship with God and with each other. Given the implicit theology of these authors, it is no wonder that the pastors they create in their stories have no hope, no possibility of redemption.

Many of us have grown up with a view of conversion as a one-time, sudden encounter with God. But most of us also realize that we, although converted, are not transformed into the image of Christ or any image of perfection immediately, if ever in this life. While the converted are reckoned as righteous, in right relationship, in the eyes of God, in everyday life we have to cultivate and seek the love and forgiveness of other people.

This means that our sins and shortcomings may never fully go away; they, instead, can resurface, not to punish us, but to help us gain a deeper healing and a more profound experience of grace that enables us to enter into a more significant relationship with God and other people. John Wesley in his sermon entitled "On the Deceitfulness of the Human Heart" says:

> Only let it be remembered, that the heart, even of a believer, is not wholly purified when he is justified. Sin is then overcome, but it is not rooted out; it is conquered, but not destroyed. Experience shows him, First, that the roots of sin, self-will, pride, and idolatry remain still in his heart. But as long as he continues to watch and pray, none of them can prevail against him.[5]

Justification refers to the grace of God that puts the sinner in a right relationship with God, and Wesley saw this as part of the salvation process. Thus, Wesley provides another conversation that helps Christians understand that the work of salvation is never complete. This ongoing work of grace originates with God and is called sanctification.

As indicated, the conversation involving inner healing is grounded in a theology of sanctification. Conversion or personal salvation is based on God's unmerited grace that impacts and transforms a person's life. Yet, conversation is also a result of God's wooing us, courting us, or even luring us to want to have a relationship with God at all. This grace that "goes before" is called prevenient grace. So even from the beginning, God is there for us, and there is no part of living that needs to fall outside of God's care. God's grace is sufficient for all of our needs.

The progression of prevenient, justifying, to sanctifying grace mirrors our human relationship with God as our faith develops and as we are spiritually formed into the image of Christ. But Wesley was also adamant that personal holiness was not only a private, internal affair, because it also entails service (acts of justice and mercy) toward others. Personal growth can involve revisiting past problems as an opportunity for not only personal growth and development but for the community's growth and development as well.

Spiritual Renewal Models for Clergy

This section will present a model of spiritual renewal and growth that will help clergy go beyond the one-time conversion model. The one-time model severely limits the growth possibilities of persons because it is grounded in a view of human perfection that is unrealistic. Rather than seeing perfection as an ongoing lifelong process, one-time conversion makes perfection complete at conversion. Such a limited view sets up unnecessary internal conflict for clergy, as exemplified by Rev. Phillip Martin. Thus a model of growing into perfection, not perfection itself, is the goal. The aim is faithful service to God through responding to God's ever-present grace.

I will present two models to help clergy grow in responsible grace. The first was initially introduced in my book *Recalling Our Own Stories: Spiritual Renewal for Religious Caregivers*.[6] The second is based on Michael White's concept of definitional ceremony.[7] Both models are based on the premise that exploring the nature of internalized conversations is fundamental to our growth and development. More precisely, internalized conversations form the convictions, values, and beliefs we have about ourselves, our relationships with others, and the world in general.

Recalling Our Own Stories is intended to help religious leaders explore their internalized beliefs and convictions. Learning to reconnect with our internalized conversation is the systematic process of examining those beliefs and convictions we develop over the years and determining the impact that these beliefs and convictions have on our current behavior.[8]

The process involves returning to our earliest memories as a way to recover some of the earliest conversations that we internalized.[9] The next dimension of the process involves attending to our birth stories, which also provide clues into some of the earliest conversations that have shaped our lives. Following this the process examines our birth order in the family, the beliefs and convictions surrounding our gender, how we were assigned our names and nicknames, the nature of our relationships with our siblings, the roles we played in our families of birth, and how we were disciplined. These dimensions of the process are intended to help the religious person identify the conversations that inform his or her current beliefs and convictions about life and ministry.

The process also involves exploring the conversations the religious caregiver internalized from the family of origin. This involves conversations about ideal mate images, ideal family images, and ideal child images that affected the development of the religious caregiver.[10] Finally, the exploration concludes with the conversations that shape the religious caregiver's understanding of ministry. Such an exploration includes remembering one's call and the circumstances surrounding it, how ministry influences one's self-esteem, how one feels about and around authority figures, the roles one plays, and the stories that inform ministry.

The goal of such exploration is to help the religious caregiver bring the conversation informing his or her behavior into the open. Once these conversations have been identified, they can be edited, re-authored, modified, upgraded, downgraded, or discarded. The basic assumption is that we can change the influence of the conversations that have shaped our lives.

The Definitional Ceremony

The idea of the definitional ceremony is to actively impact the conversations that are shaping a person's life through a process of storytelling, re-storytelling, and retelling the retelling of the story. This idea of impacting the conversations that have shaped people's lives is developed in the thinking of Michael White.[11] The purpose of the definitional ceremony is to introduce options and to present alternative forums and different practices so that persons can learn new conversations.[12] This process also involves remembering past conversations.

The process calls for an affirmative audience whose task is to listen to the stories of individuals who are willing to tell them. Oftentimes these stories are problem laden. If these storytellers are clergy, they often tell stories about work-related situations. The audience listens carefully and is given instructions to attend not only to the story but also to the associations that the story triggers. Following the telling of the story by the storyteller, the leader of the group instructs members of the audience to retell the story that they have just heard using some of the associations that they made. The original storyteller becomes part of the listening audience. The original storyteller is given the instruction to listen carefully to the retelling. She or he is also told to pay attention to the associations that the retelling creates within him or her. After about four or five persons share retellings, the original storyteller is told to retell the story taking into consideration what she or he heard from the retelling.

A vivid example of the use of the definitional ceremony process was experienced with a group of African American pastors. I was asked to help pastors deal with their personal issues. I told the story of Rev. Martin as found in Ernest Gaines's novel *In My Father's House*. At first the pastors wanted to analyze the nature of Rev. Martin's problem and found it difficult to bring out their own issues. Then, one person volunteered to tell what was going on in his church.

What the person communicated was that people in the church were resisting the institution of new programs. In fact, several of the church members were so upset that they called a special meeting to bring the pastor in line. This disturbed and disheartened the pastor. Rather than processing the story in the traditional way I had been taught, I asked members of the group who wanted to to retell the story so that if anyone wanted to give prescriptions about what they thought the person needed to do, they would have to put their advice in the retelling.

Five persons volunteered to retell the story. All were different, but they included clues that the original storyteller could use. The retelling also forced those persons to use bits and pieces of their own stories and how they had faced similar situations. When all five finished, I asked the original storyteller to retell the story again; however, I asked the storyteller to include insights learned from hearing the others.

By the time the original storyteller finished, a transformation had taken place. The person was able to discern insights that helped him upgrade the story and gain some perspective on what was happening. The process of learning and editing the original story was quite remarkable.

The original storyteller was able to retell the story in ways that brought insight to his personal problem, because he was able to finally be free from the stories his parents had created for him. After retelling the story, he realized that the same thing was taking place in his church. The church was like his parents in that it was trying to recruit him into a story that he could not adopt. Thus, the person, with the help of the group, identified the problem, and he was free to decide just how to deal with the church situation.

Sometimes the original storyteller is not ready to retell the retelling of the story. In one instance where the original storyteller was not ready, someone from the audience including the leader became a substitute for the original storyteller so that the original storyteller could visualize the process at work. This provides some safety and lessens the anxiety for not only the original storyteller but the entire group as well.

Conclusion

To help hurting ministers become whole persons, this chapter discussed two views of conversion that lead to different kinds of conversation with God. The first is a static one-time view of conversion. This view typically emphasizes a dramatic event with a transformed and redirected life, but leaves no room for further spiritual growth and development. This conversion may lead to conversation with God, but it precludes the possibility of a continual and deepening relationship with God. This type of conversation characterizes the lives of clergy in the novels discussed in this chapter.

The second type of conversion is not dependent on a one-time event because it recognizes the continual desire God has for conversation with us. Likewise when conversion becomes a reality, the person's relationship with God and conversation with God further facilitates spiritual growth and development. Conversation with God is ongoing and renewing. Values, convictions, and beliefs that inform life are also continually renewed in light of an ongoing and deepening relationship with God.

To facilitate dynamic, growth-oriented conversation with God, this chapter illustrated two models that are especially helpful for clergy so that clergy can move beyond being problems to themselves and others to being better able to care for others.

Notes

1. Ernest J. Gaines, *In My Father's House* (New York: Vintage Contemporaries, 1992), 69.

2. Randy L. Maddox, *Responsible Grace: John Wesley's Practical Theology* (Nashville: Kingswood Books, 1994), 235-36.

3. Pearl Cleage, *What Looks Like Crazy on an Ordinary Day* (New York: Anchor Books, 1997).

4. Gloria Naylor, *The Men of Brewster Place* (New York: Hyperion, 1998).

5. *The Works of John Wesley*, Volume 7 (Grand Rapids Mich.: Baker Books, 1996), 341.

6. Edward P. Wimberly, *Recalling Our Own Stories: Spiritual Renewal for Religious Caregivers* (San Francisco: Jossey-Bass, 1999).

7. Michael White, *Re-Authoring Lives: Interviews and Essays* (Adelaide, South Australia: Dulwich Centre Publications, 1998) and *Narratives of Therapists' Lives* (Adelaide, South Australia: Dulwich Centre Publications, 1997).

8. Wimberly, *Recalling Our Own Stories*, 4.

9. Ibid., 29-33. See this reference for the questions that are involved in reconnecting.

10. Ibid., 55-58.

11. See White, *Narratives of Therapists' Lives*, 93-118.

12. Ibid., 4.

CHAPTER SIX

THE PRACTICE OF CONVERSATION

Linguistic-Narrative Theories

Certain assumptions undergird the understanding of conversation presented here. Some assumptions are theological, and they will be explored in the following chapter. Other assumptions are theoretical and come from what is called a linguistic-narrative orientation to understanding human behavior. My approach to conversation in this book proceeds on many of the assumptions operative in the linguistic-narrative orientation with particular attention given to the work of Michael White. Michael White, in turn, builds much of his theory on the work of Michel Foucault; therefore, this chapter will focus on the work of these two men.

Michael White

For Michael White liberation and therapy are intertwined. White sees himself facilitating human freedom and using his profession of marriage and family therapy to accomplish this goal. The major task, then, of therapy is to free human beings from the negative stories into which they have been recruited early in their lives so that they can find authentic ways to story their experiences that can give their lives more meaning and vitality. Living out stories that others have shaped for us, he believes, demeans us and makes it difficult to live fruitfully and meaningfully. Therefore, therapy enables people to participate in the formation of their own stories so that they may live authentically.[1]

Put in psychological language, the capacity to participate in the stories that shape one's own life is called *agency*. White assumes that the capacity to create meaning is basic to being human and can be expanded to increase authentic living. Authentic living refers to creating personal stories that not only reflect one's own past history of story creating but also represents one's own uniqueness. Thus, his theories underscore the importance of the individual. This uniqueness means being free from stories imposed by others and, at the same time, being able to transform inherited stories into one's own autobiography. Thus, the telos of maturity is the ability to define oneself by becoming free from imposed definitions of the self, and the capacity to redefine and re-author the self.[2]

The point is that White's work involves the liberation of the self, which involves power and politics. Power involves the ability to create meaning, and politics deal with imposed meaning on the lives of others. Liberation involves the power to overcome the oppressive and subjugating effects of being recruited into stories and problems into which one is recruited.[3]

The Theory of Practice

One of the core concepts that White uses to talk about the task of re-authoring lives is practice. For example, he uses the terms *therapeutic practices*, *relational practices*, and *the practices of the self*.[4] He uses the term *practice* primarily as an activity in which one participates that orients that person to the language and conversational environments in which he or she participates. Here he emphasizes that professionals are shaped by the practices in which they engage, and often these practices alienate professionals from their authentic selves and stories. Thus, he is interested in helping professionals return to those practices that privilege the voice of the professional individual rather than the voices of the profession.[5]

The Definition of Practice in the Work of Michel Foucault

White borrows the concept of practice from Michel Foucault, philosopher and historian of language.[6] For Foucault, *practice* refers to certain activities that take place within a particular professional environment. Practice proceeds on the basis of set rules that give order and meaning to objects, activities, and relationships. Practice is important because it helps the professional perceive reality in a certain way, particularly through human discourse or conversation. Thus, practice shapes the reality of the professional's life through human conversation. As the professional practices within a particular place and context, she or he is being formed into a professional as well as to being shaped into a particular understanding of reality.

For Foucault, practice establishes for the professional what is real, what is appropriate, what is acceptable, what are the norms, and what are the criteria for relating to others. It sanctions certain activities and provides attribution and language categories, as well as a set of skills and knowledge. Thus, practice helps the professional determine what is significant and meaningful within a certain environment.

The site at which practice takes place is very important for Foucault. It is the site, location, or context that brings meaning and significance to the practice,[7] because it is the discourses or conversations that take place within the setting that shape reality for the professional. Foucault pays particular attention to the medical environment, especially the hospital, laboratory, and the clinical setting.

Foucault also talks about the practices of self-care.[8] He is interested in the history of self-care in antiquity as a cultural practice informing how people would go about caring for themselves physically, emotionally, spirituality, and interpersonally. Thus, he points out that self-care in Greek and Roman culture was a moral standard and had a very high priority. It was an obligation. Self-wisdom was a must. Therefore, the practices of self included introspection, self-examination, self-reflection, remembering, use of spiritual guides, attending to conversation between the body and the soul, high moral living, practicing abstinence as a form of self-development, and self-control.

I need also to say something more about the concept of discourse. For Foucault, human discourse, or conversation that takes place within particular settings, has the power to shape reality for the professional. The context of the discourse orients everything that the professional does.

Discourse proceeds on the basis of certain repeated statements, and these statements then form systems of meaning that inform the professional's view of life and death, ethical choices, therapeutic practices, teaching models, and knowledge. Thus, within certain settings selective discourse or conversations are privileged or are valued over other conversations, and attending to these selective privileged conversations shape what it means to be professional.

A final word needs to be said about discourse and conversation. For Foucault, discourse is itself a practice. As a practice, discourse privileges certain conversations over other conversations. Thus, the making of meaning is primarily a social undertaking within a particular context.

Practice in the Thought of Michael White

Michael White says that the professional practices of therapists often alienate the therapists themselves. For White a consequence of their practice is that they get burned out and lose themselves. His goal then is to introduce new practices that will liberate therapists from these practices.

From a developmental point of view, White deals with adults. His concern is with the already formed individual and the way that individual has been shaped and formed by practices that have already occurred. These practices have taken place as the result of certain activities within the family, extended family, school, religious setting, and other face-to-face conversations. Thus, White does not spend as much time dealing with how conversations were initially internalized in early childhood. He simply assumes that adults bring already formed internalized conversations into the therapeutic setting that need to be addressed.

As a family therapist in the narrative tradition, White attends more to the cognitive aspects of the story than to the unconscious dimensions of the story. He emphasizes that human beings have the capacity to create meaning as they participate in the ongoing conversations with others. Thus, change comes more from participation in conversations and stories and from examining how one has been recruited into stories that are not compatible with the self.

Addressing internalized conversations that adults bring into therapy and the clinical setting is called *externalization*. Externalization increases personal agency and the creation of one's sense of self by exploring the ways that the self has been formed and shaped by stories and conversations dominated by others.[9] Persons, including practitioners, who come to therapy bring with them problem-laden issues related to certain truths about themselves, their character, their nature, and purposes that dominate their lives. Thus, they have internalized conversations that do not facilitate growth and that prevent them from becoming a fully authentic self. In order to grow and move toward full authenticity, they need to externalize such conversations in such a way that identifies and maps them out. Once these conversations have been identified along with the activities that have formed them, the person is free to update, downgrade, edit, re-author, or discard the internalized conversations in favor of other conversations.

White uses the concept of *deconstruction* to describe the process of externalization.[10] Internalized conversations become truths that captivate the individual's life. Thus, the practice of deconstruction is the process of exploring the history of how certain truths have become established in one's life. In fact, White views the process of deconstruction as one that explores how one has been recruited into certain truths about who one is. For White recruiting is the practice of power where persons are drawn into stories about themselves that they have not created.[11] For example, White talks about persons who have been recruited into negative identities because they have been engaged in well-established patterns of self-abuse learned in abusive settings. More precisely, "These persons are engaging in conversations with self and with others that internalize the locus of abuse, and, with this, there can be no appreciation of context."[12] Therefore externalizing this power process de-politicizes it so that a re-politicizing process can begin. *Re-politicizing* refers to taking the process of defining the self away from others and placing it within oneself.

The community is essential when persons are externalizing conversations that have been internalized. White believes that stories persons have internalized are the result of participating in community with others; therefore, it makes sense to engage communities of persons in the process of externalization or what White calls "the renegotiation of identity."[13] Those who make up the communities for the renegotiation of identity are an audience who can help authenticate new and preferred truths about the self as they emerge during therapy.[14]

Another term for externalization is *re-storying*.[15] White believes that life is multistoried and that there are dominant stories as well as *substories*.[16] He thinks that substories are available and are an excellent reservoir of potential for re-storying individuals, couples, and families. In fact, he believes that there are latent experiences that have not been given full expression in either the dominant story or the substory that can form the basis for re-storying. As one learns to privilege various aspects of the substories by reflecting on them, playing with them, conversing about them, and evaluating them, one begins the re-storying process.

From exploring latent possibilities in the substories, it is possible to ground one's identity in a new plot.[17] It is naming a counterplot or alternative plot, in White's mind. A plot gives direction and meaning to one's life, and it is the plot that shapes one's memory. So positive stories yield positive plots and negative stories yield negative plots. Thus re-storying assists the emergence of a counterplot that gives life new meaning.

Re-storying is a practice. This means that within the process of therapy, persons map the influence of the internalized stories on their lives. Others, including the therapist and other companions in the therapeutic journey, provide an audience for authenticating a new emergent identity. New conversations take the place of old ones. Negative, maladaptive, or painful discourses are overthrown and reworked so that a fresh growth-facilitating plot can begin to emerge.

The Practice of Re-Storying in Therapists' Lives

One of the problems that accompany professional training according to White is the loss of self with resulting burnout. Therapists are prone to burnout because they are trained to ignore the knowledge and skill acquired in their experiences prior to their professional training. Consequently White believes that it is important to address practices that help shape the professional psychotherapist. These practices include the practices of therapy and the practices of the self.

Significant for the development of the self prior to professional training is what White calls local discourses. Local discourses represent those original conversations that generate our first sense of what it means to be a professional.[18] Related concepts are lay communities and affiliating networks. From these communities we learn to privilege certain knowledge and skills that often become authentic parts of the self. When membership in such communities facilitate the emergence of an authentic self and have not recruited the professional into negative stories, the knowledge and skills that have been learned in these communities cannot and should not be ignored.[19] Thus, these, perhaps original memberships and related discourses are essential for the further development of the professional.

White believes that professional training for psychotherapists is often alienating. In fact, he believes that professional education often alienates persons from those important conversations and practices that have previously shaped them. Even further, he thinks that professional education often dishonors the local folk knowledge that has been learned in local memberships.[20] He writes:

> As lives become professionally membered in the monoculture of psychotherapy, and in the dishonoring of the memberships through which local and folk knowledges have been co-generated through personal history, much is forsaken. The outcome for many is a dis-membership that contributes to a loss of history, and a loss of a particular sense of self. It is also a dis-membership that deprives persons of the opportunity to join locally with others in connecting the specific experiences of their lives (including their work) to the shared values and beliefs that are privileged in different communities of persons, and to experience so doing in relation to the significant themes and meanings of life.[21]

The concept of membership and dismembership are introduced above; *membership* refers to our original meaning-making environment and *dismembership* is alienation from it. White believes that professional education alienates persons from these important sources of knowledge and skill; therefore, he introduces the concept of re-membership as one that can provide the practices and processes for the formation of the therapist. *Re-membership* is the practice of providing forums of authenticity where therapists-in-training are given affirming audiences who can acknowledge the legacies that trainees bring with them. In this way what the student brings becomes part of the educational process in a nonalienating way.[22] Thus, *re-membering* or remembering assists the process of agency or co-construction of the professional identity of the therapist in a way that adds meaning and prevents burnout and loss of self.

A good example of re-membership was in my training in pastoral counseling training at the Danielsen Institute at Boston University. The background of the Danielsen Center is in the psychoanalytic tradition. In order to show myself competent in this tradition, I attempted to become a good psychoanalyst. I had two years of pastoral counseling supervision prior to entering the Danielsen Institute, and I thought that I had mastered this particular style. After sixth months, there was a review of my performance, and they concluded that what I was doing on the tape was not truly who I was. They wanted me to integrate who I was more into how I carried out my counseling. They felt I needed to become more myself and use the natural gifts that I had.

The point is that I was expected to engage who I was as a person into my style of pastoral counseling. I was not expected to do away with what I had brought to the training events. I was to integrate it with what I was learning so that I could develop an authentic style.

The real danger in discarding what we bring to professional education is that much of our effectiveness rests in our personhood. Disengaging from what we bring to professional training eventually makes us ineffective in our attempt to help others to develop who they are. We have to practice the re-membership in order to help others to be authentic selves and connect with what they bring to the task of living. Much of authentic living is discovering what already exists within us that is vital for developing meaning. This is accomplished best when we can model this form of connecting in what we do and say ourselves.

Disconnecting from our original selves and the knowledge and skills associated with our original learning contexts also could lead to loss of self. The critical concern is that we can only endure trying to be something we are not for a short period of time. Eventually, we must attend to our hidden selves and reunite with them in order for our lives to be meaningful. The midlife crisis is often the place where neglected aspects of ourselves get reconnected so that we can face the future with creativity and purpose.

There are also other practices that White feels are important in facilitating human agency for professionals and nonprofessionals. People need settings where they can reclaim knowledge in significant relational associations. For White these are definitional ceremonies. A *definitional ceremony* is a structured forum of acknowledgment where one can discover alternative practices in the presence of witnesses. These settings become authenticating forums of participation where new knowledge and skills are learned.[23] Such forums include a process of storytelling, retelling of the story, and retelling of the retelling. (See chapter 5 for an explanation of this process.)

While the practices of re-membership and of the definitional ceremony are related to efforts to change internal conversations, White has a lot to say about the practice of internalization of negative conversations in particular. He talks about the practices of self-subjugation. These practices bespeak the power inherent in relationships where people learn to subordinate and undermine their own lives. Subjugation practices begin with being recruited into negative stories of others. Such stories are then internalized so that they result in rigorous self-surveillance, self-punishments for transgressions, negative self-evaluations, self-denial, and self-imposed exile. White calls these phenomena the negative practices of self.[24]

Related to the practices of self-subjugation are the practices of totalization or labeling.[25] White thinks that people are often recruited and labeled in ways that become a self-fulfilling prophecy. The goal of such totalizing is to get the person to self-impose oppression so that external oppressive structures are not needed.

Not only does White feel that people can get recruited, he also believes that pathologizing conversations contribute to the totalization of those who are mentally ill. He says that many people bring problems to therapy that are the result of inequality in gender, race, ethnicity, class, and age.[26] He takes seriously the role of power and its ability to set in motion certain discourses that have the ability to undermine the self-esteem of people. Further, he says that therapeutic practices should have as one of their goals the dismantling of structures of inquality.[27]

Therapeutic Conversation

White subjects the practice of psychotherapy to his analysis of discourse. For him, psychotherapy is a powerful meaning-making vehicle that has the awesome potential to subjugate those who come for healing.

White believes that the therapeutic conversation should not become the place where the counselee learns the language of therapy. Therapeutic language should not dominate the counselee's world. He believes that the context of counseling should be the conversational context that shapes the counselee's life and internal conversations.[28] Because the therapist is almost always a representative of power, the conversations within the therapeutic relationship often overshadow the conversations taking place in the everyday world of the counselee.[29] Thus, the original knowledge learned by the counselee can be marginalized and treated as unimportant. In this way, the therapeutic process contributes to undermining practices of the self. To avoid the negative result, White writes that the practice of psychotherapy should always keep its focus on the conversations that the counselee brings to counseling. Thus, re-membering conversational practices, storytelling, retelling the storytelling and retelling of the retelling practices, structuring feedback forums, and creating settings for practices of acknowledgment help keep the focus of therapy on conversations that the counselee brings to therapy.[30] Consequently, the privileging of conversation involves focusing on what emerges in the life of the counselee; therapeutic language or jargon does not.

As indicated earlier, White focuses on the cognitive dimension that makes up the conversation more than on the unconscious processes of the ego defending itself or resisting growth. His approach assumes readiness and eagerness of those involved to explore alternative conversations. He assumes that the person has moved beyond the stage of resistance and is actively engaged in pursuing life goals and more preferred scenarios for living. Thus, his narrative means to therapeutic ends assume that attending to stories and conversations either works despite the defenses or that the person is nodefensive.

Conclusion

This chapter set out to examine some of the theoretical assumptions undergirding the concept of conversation. As human beings we learn by internalizing certain conversations, and from these conversations and stories we find direction for our lives. Thus, meaning comes from the process of discourse.

Though it might seem that certain discourses in our culture are dominant and that we are passive recipients of what our cultural language system presents, we have an active part. We have the capacity to help shape the way we practice conversations. Though we can be recruited into negative stories and conversations, we are never totally at their mercy. We can increase our capacity for privileging conversations. It is the role of therapy to help us learn to privilege conversations in ways that contribute to our growth and development and to limit those internal conversations that have subjugated us.

Developmentally, we are dependent upon our original meaning-making environment in our significant relationships. As adults we gain more and more power to edit those conversations that continue to shape our lives. Moreover, we don't stop internalizing conversation as adults. A difficult childhood does not have to condemn us to a traumatic adulthood. We continue to grow and develop throughout adulthood. For example, we internalize professional conversations that the practices of our professions and work provide. Such practices proceed on the basis of the rules of discourse related to their particular environment. These rules form groups of coherent or related statements that make up systems of meaning that inform what we do in our work.

Even though the professional and other workers learn their identities through practice, they cannot discard what they initially bring to their jobs from their original meaning-making environments. To do so would be self-sabotaging and self-subjugating. One must enter into the dialogue the knowledge and skills one learned in the original meaning-making environment with professional/work conversations. In such engagements the person can then decide whether to upgrade, downgrade, discard, or re-edit what they brought into the work environment. Thus, human agency or one's participation in meaning-making increases.

The concept of practice involved in professional discourse has proved very helpful in my analysis of the novels used in this book particularly in the discussion of how clergy need to engage with what they bring to conversations theologically. In the cases presented, the clergy needed to upgrade their theological folk wisdom. I also suggested that the practice of re-membering was a place to start. The old conversations were grounded in the popular cultural notion that behavioral perfection and inner spiritual maturing were once-and-for-all results of conversion. Such a view says that further spiritual and emotional growth are not necessary at all. This makes it difficult for pastors to adequately respond to difficult situations that arise, particularly from the past. Therefore a process of reviewing life-shaping theological conversations had to take place if the pastors were to grow and learn from past mistakes.

Privileging God conversation is a process that is learned in the practice of human and divine discourse. Just as Job learned to privilege conversation with God, so can we. Job first engaged in conversations with his peers who embodied the legacy of traditional wisdom. When their individual and collective wisdom failed to help Job deal with his current circumstances, he was forced to examine past conversations in light of his desire to hear from God. When he did hear what God had to say, Job found ways to allow these conversations to shape him over against other conversations that had informed both him and his culture.

In the novels, we saw how God conversation took place in the lives of everyday people. Certain images, ideas, sayings, pictures, memories, epiphanies, and so forth, increased the characters' awareness of the importance of the spiritual realm. Those having these types of experiences found various ways to enter into the process of allowing them to inform their lives. The experiences may have come and gone, but their impact continued to mold the characters over time.

The fact that God conversation exists and can be a central reality in shaping persons' identity must be taken seriously. In fact, contemporary novels reflect an undercurrent of spirituality that is taking place in our culture. Spirituality is back on center stage, and learning to privilege the conversations we have as the result of our spiritual experience is very important.

There is no doubt that there is room for great deception in regard to conversation with God. This is why I believe in checking what we hear in conversations against the conversation we hear in participating in our faith traditions. This is the method of coherence where the participation in faith traditions allows us to check out our conversations in light of conversations within the church. One reason communities of faith exist is to validate and perpetuate God's narrative with God's people. Self-deception is more difficult if the faith community operates in this way. Privileging God conversation is real, but it is not a blinding process. It helps us to be realistic about what we internalize. God conversation challenges false images and false conversation. Moreover, God conversation is a process taking place over long periods of time. Thus, God conversation helps us to test what we internalize. We must engage in it with our eyes and the eyes of caring others, past and present, wide open.

Notes

1. This chapter reflects on the following works of Michael White: Michael White and D. Epston, *Narrative Means to Therapeutic Ends* (New York: Norton, 1990); *Narratives of Therapists' Lives* (Adelaide, South Australia: Dulwich, 1997); *Re-Authoring Lives: Interviews and Essays* (Adelaide, South Australia: Dulwich, 1995).

2. White, *Re-Authoring Lives,* 48.

3. Michel Foucault, *The Care of Self: The History of Sexuality,* Vol. 3 (New York: Vintage Books, 1988), 39-68. See also White, *Re-Authoring Lives,* 41-49.

4. White, *Narratives of Therapists' Lives,* vi-viii.

5. Ibid., 3-4.

6. Michel Foucault, *The Archaeology of Knowledge and The Discourse on Language* (New York: Pantheon Books, 1972), 46-49.

7. Ibid., 54-55.

8. Foucault, *The Care of Self,* 39-68.

9. White, *Re-Authoring Lives*, 22-23.
10. Ibid., 24.
11. Ibid., 48-49.
12. Ibid., 48.
13. Ibid., 26.
14. Ibid., 27.
15. Ibid.
16. Ibid., 27-28.
17. Ibid., 28-29.
18. White, *Narratives of Therapists' Lives*, 10-11.
19. Ibid., 12.
20. Ibid., 17.
21. Ibid., 17-18.
22. Ibid., 13-16.
23. Ibid., 4.
24. White, *Re-Authoring Lives*, 44-45.
25. Ibid., 49.
26. Ibid., 115.
27. Ibid., 116.
28. White, *Narratives of Therapists' Lives*, 200.
29. Ibid., 201.
30. Ibid., 202.

CHAPTER SEVEN

THE SECOND INNOCENCE

Privileging God Conversation in Job

The thoughts of the biblical book of Job have shaped our understanding of privileging conversation, particularly conversation with God. Our discussion thus far has drawn on the wisdom of Job at key points in each chapter of this book to give a theological focus. In the relevant chapters I have shown how the plot and character development of some modern literary novels resemble some of the patterns in Job. Indeed, the conversations found in Job prefigure or set the pattern for much of the church's discourse in response to suffering. Such a pattern can become mimetic repetition for us when meaning is constructed through creatively transfiguring past patterns. This means that past patterns help people in contemporary contexts bring personal and creative meaning to their conversations.[1] This chapter will elaborate in greater detail the pattern of conversation found in the book of Job.

Fellowship and Sanctification: The Central Metaphors

The metaphors that will give shape to this discussion of Job with regard to conversation are *fellowship* and *sanctification*. Fellowship refers to a close and intimate relationship with God, which is initiated and sustained by God. It is a gift that God offers despite the ravages of suffering and pain. It is offered to all despite race, gender, or sexual orientation. Moreover, it is given as a gift of God regardless of merit. It is a free gift, and as a result of fellowship, our worth and value as human beings are a direct result of God's gift of fellowship.

Sanctification refers to the process of becoming holy, which results from growing in God's grace. Grace is an abundant reservoir of love and mercy that is a free gift of God, mediated through fellowship with God. This grace is not only a personal gift to individuals, it is to be shared with others. The sharing is modeled after Jesus' example of agape love, and it comes as a response to the grace that we have received as the result of being in fellowship with God. Sanctification is a derivative of privileging fellowship with God, and we take on the task of imitating Jesus' agape love because of the love God shows by inviting us into fellowship.

Sanctification is also related to redemptive suffering in the world. It is a partnership with God as God redeems the world. When we accept God's gift of fellowship, we are drawn not only into the benefits of God's love and mercy as well as the gift of sacred identity, but also into the cosmic conflict between God and Satan. God seems to invite us into this conflict knowing that God's fellowship and sustaining love will enable us to be victorious. Moreover, God permits Satan to challenge us knowing that partnership with God in redeeming a fallen world does involve the suffering of the righteous. Like Job, however, God makes sure that our sacred worth and our meaning in life remain intact as we participate in the redemptive process. Thus, accepting fellowship with God brings with it reward as well as the challenges of ministry and vocation.

African American Christians have benefited from this understanding of fellowship and sanctification in its dealing with the manifold losses due to discrimination, injustice, and prejudice. Fellowship with God has provided us dignity and honor in the midst of suffering, shame, and loss. Like Job, we have refused to take ourselves out of relationship with God. We would not give up. Though it is hard to understand God and what being in relationship with God brings, we have steadfastly trusted our relationship with God knowing that a word from God would make all the difference in the world. The result of such tenacious holding on to fellowship with God has enabled us to be victorious, rather than victims of racism and suffering. Constant dialogue with God has strengthened us, sustained us, and enabled us to make creative contributions to liberation and community.

Indeed, fellowship with God has buttressed our sacred identity as the result of our privileging our fellowship and conversation with God. Thus, our sacred identity as a gift from God has resulted in our being active and not passive; in our resisting being recruited into negative, shameful, and hurtful conversations; in continued spiritual growth, being active partners with God in redeeming the world; and being associated with the righteous cause of justice and liberation. Thus, sacred identity formation takes place as we partner with God and bring our faith community into partnership with God. Indeed, we have a unique history that draws on the interpretation of Job for our contemporary life and victorious living in the midst of suffering, injustice, and pain.

While the interpretation of Job does not answer the question of why African Americans have had to suffer the devastation of slavery, injustice, and racism, it does provide us a way to live victoriously. We know what Job knows. We know that God is faithful and will always be on time in showing up in the midst of our struggle. We have confidence in the unfolding of God's plan of salvation. We know that our redeemer is alive. It may appear that God is slaying us, but we know we can trust that God is working the plot of God's story to redeem the world. We know that we are becoming holy in the process of faithfulness to God and being faithful in sharing God's grace with others.

Prefiguring, Configuring, Transfiguring

As African American Christians, privileging the model of Job as a way to derive meaning in the midst of suffering, injustice, and racism developed over time. We had to enter into the story of Job through hearing and reading it as individuals and as communities of faith. As we heard the story of Job over and over again, we identified with Job's plight and saw that it was similar to our own. Through identifying with his plight we also identified with the plot that undergirded Job's story, and we developed the expectation that the plot that gave meaning to his life would give meaning to our life.[2] We also had to live out the plot as well undergo the same process as Job. We had to experience the frustration of using contemporary and inherited wisdom to understand our suffering. In fact, we had been provided a perspective from the slave masters and purveyors of racism into which we had been recruited. Yet, we realized that this meaning into which we had been recruited was not only false but also inadequate to liberate us and bring victory into our lives. Thus, our slave parents had to wait on the unfolding of God's plot to bring the kind of meaning that would liberate.

From the point of view of mimetic repetition, the experience of suffering is the experience or event that triggers the need for understanding. *Prefiguring* means experience prior to understanding or having meaning. In narrative terms prefiguring foreshadows understanding; *configuring* means to give experience meaning. With regard to suffering, configuration is the point of using past meaning to understand the current experience of suffering. *Transfiguration* is the creative process of making sense of the experience of suffering, drawing on modified inherited wisdom. The point is that the person experiencing suffering must make sense of it, so there is a creative dimension in using the inherited wisdom in this process. Inherited wisdom cannot just be adopted without some creative tailoring for the present.

Applied to the book of Job, privileging conversations occurs in stages, beginning with prefiguring, moving to configuring, and finally to transfiguring; each of these stages is a process within itself. In Job we also see a view of suffering as corrective punishment, for sin was an important idea upon which Job drew, but it was not sufficient to help him understand what he was experiencing. Therefore, he had to transform the wisdom he had inherited by necessity in ways that could help him make sense of his current experience of suffering.

From a theological point of view, the book of Job is an extended conversation within which Job's prosperous and honorable life is disrupted through the ravages of suffering and pain. He brings to this experience a cultural and religious wisdom of his place and time that sees suffering as God's punishment for sin. Gradually, he finds this understanding totally inadequate. Through a process of entering into conversations with others and finally with God, Job is able to transform his view of suffering. He begins to view it as a condition of life that God can use to redeem the world. Thus, he transforms or creatively edits the received wisdom tradition to create a new understanding of God as companion in partnership and fellowship despite suffering and pain. He refuses to be further recruited into the prevailing wisdom, and he becomes a very active participant in creating a new understanding of living in the world despite the presence of suffering. In his active participation in creating new meaning, he discovers that vocation and ministry must take place in the midst of suffering and pain. That is to say that his role as leader in the community had to take on new meaning; to be a leader in Job's day one had to have honor based on material success. Thus, Job had to revision his understanding of being a leader who suffered shame in the eyes of the community. Privileging God conversation enabled him to eventually transcend the conventional wisdom into which he was recruited and to replace it with a thought process that included hopeful meaning despite suffering.

To continue the discussion of privileging conversation with God, I will focus on various themes from Job's conversations. Key themes are the notion of lament as pursuit of God, redemptive suffering versus remedial suffering, honor and shame in ancient wisdom, and apocalyptic dualism of time as a pattern for contemporary theology.

Lament as Pursuit of God

> Oh, that I knew where I might find him,
>   that I might come even to his dwelling!
> I would lay my case before him
>   and fill my mouth with arguments.
> (Job 23:3-4)

Privileging conversation with God proceeds on the basis of making one's conversation with God primary or central above all other conversations in one's life's narrative. In the book of Job, there are several conversations, and each character in the unfolding drama is used to present different conversations about the inherited Jewish wisdom tradition as it relates to suffering. One significant conversation involves the distinction between lament and blasphemy.

Job's comforters embrace a particular understanding of how to pay respect to God and how to give reverence to God. It was considered disrespectful and hence unrighteous or sinful to blame God for suffering. Because they see Job as doing just that, being disrespectful, they have grave difficulty accepting Job's complaints; so they seek to correct Job's thinking. They seem to think that Job's negative words reflect his sin, so they use the inherited wisdom about addressing God to inform Job.

Three of Job's friends feel that his complaints against God either border on or are blasphemous. Biblically, the term *blasphemy* refers to showing contempt or a lack of reverence for God or something sacred.[3] In fact, Eliphaz, one of Job's conversation partners, accuses Job of a lack of reverence in 15:4. Eliphaz says, "but you are doing away with the fear of God,/ and hindering meditation before God." He sees Job as rebellious, therefore irreverent, toward God. Such irreverence was thought to completely alienate one from God. In fact, Eliphaz believed that Job was threatening his relationship with God or at least hindering the possibility of communing with God by committing heresy.

It is clear to me that the book of Job introduces a new understanding of God conversation. In my mind the writer introduces an understanding of lament or complaint that not only does pay reverence to God but also invites God into conversation with the complainer. Rather than destroying the relationship, the writer of Job emphasizes that this strengthens one's relationship with God.

J. Gerald Janzen points out that chapter 23 is about Job reaching out to God in loyalty and honesty, desiring to be in relationship with God.[4] Janzen's view is that Job is seeking a genuine and open relationship with God where he can bring his authentic self into fellowship with God. Job is not showing disrespect to God or even elevating himself over God; rather Job wants to enter into a fuller and deeper relationship with God. In short, the book of Job is about lament or complaint understood as outreach to God to which God responds openly. Rather than destroying a relationship with God, lament is presented as helping to facilitate God's response to human pain.

The book of Job seeks to reconfigure the received wisdom about complaint as the pursuit of God. More precisely, Job reconfigures the traditional meaning of suffering. Job's prosperity and abundance are dramatically interrupted by severe suffering and loss. As Job sorts through his true feelings, in part through dialogue with his friends, he gradually decides to engage God directly and risk alienating God. But rather than being alienated, God responds. Thus, Job's experience with God enables him to transform and to reconfigure ancient dread about the fear of God into a way of engaging God that brings added meaning to life. Thus his direct experience with God enables Job to enrich his relationship with God. The irony is, of course, that Job's rich experience of God turns the conventional wisdom upside down. The poor, bereft Job has a rich relationship with God, while his prosperous friends have an impoverished relationship with God.

Lament, then, is a form of conversation with God that can help open the door to an authentic relationship with God. Lament is human frankness and complaint about one's experience of suffering that helps one experience healing. It not only signals one's readiness to enter a new relationship with God but also flags one's willingness to receive revelation from God.

As African Americans, we not only identified with the character of Job and the underlying plot of Job's story, we also took on the lamenting role of Job. We felt abandoned by God, but we knew God would eventually make God's presence and will known. We knew we would eventually hear from God and that our lives would be more meaningful as a result. We understand that God was an on-time God who did not come when we wanted God to come, but God was on time nonetheless.

Redemptive Suffering Versus Corrective Suffering

One way to see the book of Job is as a reconfiguration of the meaning of suffering. It is also about the transformation of the meaning of corrective or remedial suffering to a new understanding of redemptive suffering. Remedial suffering is God's attempt to develop human character through punishment; redemptive suffering, however, is the inevitable consequence of partnering with God as God transforms the world. Redemptive suffering comes with the package of deciding to accept God's call to service.

In deciding to cast our lot with God, at first we are not aware what it means. We only find out later what it means to be a servant of God. It was only after Job had spent time with God in fellowship in the hedge-like condition that he discovered there was a price to pay for that relationship. In fact, there is a mimetic or repeated pattern throughout Scripture where suffering follows fellowship with God and the call to service. For example, following Jesus' baptism in Mark 1:9-12, and Matthew 3:13-4: 10, Jesus is tested by the devil. Like Job, Jesus found that fellowship with God was far more rewarding despite the challenges from the devil.

While we as African Americans can do without racism and discrimi-nation, we know that our suffering is not primarily due to our relationship with God, although we know the devil is involved. We are treated the way we are treated because of our skin color and the myths that exist as a result. Nonetheless, we find the innocent suffering of Job as a helpful story for our own situation. Being black is no crime, and therefore, we don't deserve punishment. We have a similar complaint of innocence to that of Job. In any case, however, we find that the model of redemptive suffering works knowing that fellowship and partnership with God in redeeming the world provides essential meaning for coming to grips with suffering. Yes, choosing God brings with it double jeopardy for African Americans based on race and partnership with God, yet we have discov-ered that we are far better off in relationship with God than outside of a relationship with God.

In this section I will use a narrative method to attend to the various scenes that make up the book of Job. I will explore the way the plot unfolds and discloses meaning as one engages the book.

One significant scene in the prologue of the book of Job is Satan's appearance at the heavenly gathering. This scene, as well as a later one in the prologue, reveals God permitting the inevitable plot where the devil will attack God's servants who chose fellowship with God. God realizes that the devil had been searching for opportunities to challenge God, and God provides a preemptive strike. Thus, God initiates a per-missive agreement with the devil to challenge the faithfulness of Job. Why postpone the inevitable? Therefore, God challenges Satan to involve God's servant Job. Satan accepts God's invitation and proceeds first to attack Job's possessions and family. When this fails to achieve the desired effect, Satan is given permission to attack Job's health. It is Satan's hope that these attacks will cause Job to renounce God or deny God and die. Satan seems to think that Job fears God only because God has blessed Job by making him fruitful in terms of family and possessions. So Satan believes that once he destroys Job's primary innocence and exposes him to the real world, Job will renounce God as an ineffective protector and therefore as an ineffective God. Satan further believes that Job's right relation with God hinges on what he gets from God for upholding his end of the covenant. Satan suggests to God that if God does not hold up God's end of the covenant, Job will defect rather than keep holding up his end, thus unraveling God's plan for redemption for the world.

From a narrative perspective, the agreement God enters into with Satan is a literary device to show the reality of accepting the call of copartnership with God in redeeming the world. No one lives, at least not for long, in a storybook world where tragedy is absent. From the narrator's point of view real life is lived in the midst of pain and suffering where evil abounds. The narrator's question is, Is God present in the suffering of God's people? One thing the narrator is trying to teach the community of faith is that people can live meaningful lives despite the presence of evil.

Redemptive suffering, from a narrative point of view, comes about because humans get caught in the midst of the cosmic struggle. While the book of Job may not be primarily about redemptive suffering, it is clear to me that Job's prosperity and wealth materially and relationally thrust him into being a leader in the community. As we will see in the next section, he loses this leadership role when his loses his wealth and family. As a result, he has to discover a new understanding of the meaning of leadership despite suffering. For me, Job's reconfiguring the meaning of suffering sets the pattern for the New Testament understanding of redemptive suffering. Thus, the book of Job prefigured the mimetic pattern for carrying out ministry in the midst of suffering. Therefore, Job's embracing new meaning as the result of his relationship with God also set the future pattern for New Testament redemption theology.

The writer of the book of Job reveals that secondary innocence, as I call it, is a possibility despite the presence of suffering and evil. It is possible despite being caught in the cosmic struggle. This is to say that a relationship with God is far more rewarding than material gain and possessions, because it brings a sense of peace and fulfillment in the midst of the storms of life.

Honor and Shame in Ancient Wisdom

The themes of innocence, lament, and redemptive suffering all relate to the themes of honor and shame. In the mind of Johs Pedersen, honor at the time the book of Job was written had to do with the possession of material wealth, a large family with many sons, and physical health. Such wealth and prosperity were considered to be a blessing, while not having them was considered a curse. Therefore, the book of Job when it was written was also about the need to reconfigure or transfigure the meaning of what it meant to be a person of worth and value.

Job was esteemed in his social context because people believed he was blessed by God. Job's material wealth was evidence to them that Job was a righteous man who would be further blessed by God.[5] Pedersen says:

> He is a man rich in blessing, successful in all that he undertakes. And his blessing is typically Israelic. He lives surrounded by sons, and fertility wells up around him, both in herd and the field. Milk and oil flow in currents. It is this rich blessing which creates the honor of Job. His honor, which is renewed daily, consists in being able to give.[6]

The extent to which Job is given honor is revealed in chapter 29. Chapter 29 begins with Job's remembrances of the past where he had a premier place in the public square and marketplace (verse 7). When he came into the public arena, young men withdrew and old men stood in respect (verse 8). Royalty stopped what they were doing (verse 10). He was able to respond to the needy including the fatherless and widows (verses 12-13). He was the eyes of the blind and the feet of the lame (verse 15). Job was in his glory (verse 20), and he called his existence nest-like (verse 18). In other words, Job believed his honorable status was permanent, something he would take to his grave.

But his honorable status was not permanent; his wealth and success were whisked away. Paradise gained became paradise lost. In chapter 30 Job laments the loss of his honor. He complains that people are singing mocking songs about him (verse 9). People now abhor him, spit on him, isolate him (verse 10). People now shun him; they are afraid that he will somehow contaminate them. They show no restraint in the lengths they will go to deride and ridicule him to his face (verse 11).

A bewildered Job seeks to understand what is happening. Naturally, he draws upon what has worked for him in the past—the community wisdom about honor and shame. But it doesn't work; the legacy he has to draw upon just drives him deeper into despair. He insists on his innocence. His shame is no fault of his; he has done nothing to deserve what is happening to him. Job does all he can do; he protests and laments his innocence before his friends and before God.

But despite his losses and the meaning constructs that he has inherited, Job is able to separate his value and self-worth from what the culture says it should be tied to. Job has the strength to see himself as valuable despite his society seeing him as worthless. Job never loses his positive and healthy regard of the self. When many people would have been crushed and ground beneath the heel of adversity, Job rises up and addresses his ultimate judge—God. The theological question is, Does Job's ability to withstand the worst Satan could do say something about Job or about God? I suggest it says something about both Job and God. It says that God is such an integral part of Job's being that even when God appears to be absent, God is present. In relationship to God, Job has been shaped and molded such that although defeated, Job will not be destroyed.

Many in our African American community know what it means to live in a society that does not value us. But we have discovered that God is the ultimate granter of worth and value. It is in fellowship with God that we have found our lives confirmed and our worth bestowed. It is in the "walking and talking with God" that we have found the value of privileging God conversation over all other conversations. While we would want to avoid suffering and pain related to being black or from being attacked because of siding with God, we also know that our lives are made meaningful and worthwhile because God extends God's fellowship to us. Like Job, we know that fellowship with God is far more valuable and meaningful than anything else that can be offered by the world. We can live meaningfully despite racism and evil, because we enter into relationship with God.

Indeed, Job is a mimetic pattern for us as African Americans. Job refuses to take himself out of relationship to God; he will not give up. Job is the constant, unambiguous character in the book. Job is just as God says he is, a righteous, upright person; and Job does not vary from that throughout the book. Job never becomes a passive victim. In other words, he never accepts being recruited into negative conversations nor does he have to. The writer is saying that life may be ambiguous and perhaps even God (to our understanding) is ambivalent, but we can be upright and righteous if we stay in relationship with God.

This understanding of Job really adds to our concept of God conversation. It also gives us a way to say that despite the suffering of the African American community, righteousness is a viable option. We have an opportunity to return to the original premise about sacred identity formation in a powerful way. This is what sacred identity formation yields: being active rather than passive; not having to be recruited into hurtful or shameful conversations; continued spiritual growth; being an active partner with God in redeeming the world; and maybe suffering, but for a righteous cause. Sacred identity formation takes place as one partners with God and as one brings one's faith community into partnership with God. African Americans have a unique history that speaks to the interpretation of Job for today's church and for how sacred identity formation takes place in the midst of adversity.

Notes

1. Mario J. Valdes, *Reflection and Imagination: A Ricoeur Reader* (Toronto: University of Toronto, 1991), 137-54. The understanding transfiguration is based on the three movements of mimesis. Mimesis 1 is a form of practical rationality where the first stage of meaning-making is the actual action or experience. This is called pre-configuration. Mimesis 2 is configuration where meaning is configured imitating past patterns that have provided meaning to similar experiences. Transfiguration takes place when the person brings meaning and interpretation to experience and action helped by past patterns. It is a stage of reconfiguring past patterns that adds new meaning to the present.

2. See Edward P. Wimberly, *Using Scripture in Pastoral Counseling* (Nashville: Abingdon Press, 1994), 25-27. In this book I present a model for how change comes as result of identifying with biblical stories based on similarity in context and situation.

3. Paul J. Achtemier, ed. *Harper's Bible Dictionary* (San Francisco: Harper and Row, 1985), 135.

4. J. Gerald Janzen, *Job, Interpretation: A Bible Commentary for Teaching and Preaching* (Atlanta: John Knox, 1997), 164-68.

5. Johs Pedersen, *Israel: Its Life and Culture* (London: Oxford University Press, 1964), 214-16.

6. Ibid., 214.

CHAPTER EIGHT

THE TASK OF PASTORAL COUNSELING

This final chapter is an attempt to return to the main focus of the book and to reiterate the major thesis and the insights that have emerged. The significance of such a reiteration is to help fix in our minds how we become persons of sacred worth in a culture where we are commodified and subjected to recruitment into negative and self-alienating identities. As pastoral counselors and caregivers our focus is on helping people internalize conversations that enable us to grow into whole persons with the capacity to commit ourselves to the growth of others and of community. As pastoral caregivers, we also have to help people work through internalized recruitment into negative identities fostered by a market-driven economy, the commodification of values of human worth, and the disconfirming values associated with racism and injustice. Returning to the major themes of this book will help us as pastoral counselors strategically intervene in people's lives.

From its origins, sacred identity formation is something that God does in partnership with us. It is a process whereby God, through the support of the faith community, leads us through a sorting of various cultural conversations about human worth and value until we finally reach the point of prioritizing God conversation that confirms our worth and value as God's creations. This prioritizing process is similar to the process that led to Job's transformation and his ability to feel affirmed despite the presence of evil. Likewise, African Americans continue to draw from this pattern to find meaning for our lives.

Sacred identity formation is a gift from God that is bestowed as the result of fellowship with God. In fellowship with God, not only are our worth and value established but we also learn to resist being recruited into negative identities, conversations, and stories existing in wider culture. In fellowship with God and through participation in our faith communities, we discover our own unique identities. Indeed, we are not passive recipients of conversations, stories, and societal identities. Moreover, in fellowship with God, we learn to externalize those negative and detrimental identities. As a result of this externalization, we learn to update old negative conversations as well as to internalize new conversations that facilitate growth.

As pastoral counselors and caregivers, our task is to assist persons to form sacred identities. We partner with what God is doing and with what our faith communities are doing to promote sacred identity formation. Our goal is to find the most appropriate intervention methods.

Pastoral Theology

The development of this manuscript was based on a specific pastoral theological method—the revised correlational method. The goal of this method is to develop informed insight into cultural problems or into contemporary questions that help us strategically intervene into the lives of people. Pastoral theology is oriented to the contemporary context and proceeds on the basis of critical questions that are raised and answered from both theology and social science.

This book uses modern novels to explore the theme, Why do African Americans suffer injustice? Modern novels were used to help give focus to how this question is raised in this modern context. Related questions emerging from the novels dealt with how persons found meaning and worth despite the presence of evil and their recruitment into negative racial identities. Other concerns included the contemporary images of what it means to be persons of worth and value in a market-driven culture that commodifies worth.

With the context and questions established for pastoral theology, the concern is to move systematically through a reflection process that will yield significant strategic insight. This process begins in this manuscript by using contemporary African American novelists as well. Each novel was explored for its significant questions and concerns in light of pastoral theology. This included a theoretical analysis and theological reflection on the novels with the goal of generating insight that could inform pastoral interventions. Below, these insights will be examined in light of their intervention possibilities.

Strategic Intervention

The first step in strategic intervention into people's lives is to help people address the diverse conversations occurring in their lives surrounding the concerns they present to the pastoral counselor or caregiver. Such an intervention requires a window of opportunity. A window of opportunity refers to a point in a person's life where the prevailing conversation is not adequate to provide meaning for current living. For example, in Job's life, the window of opportunity came when the ancient wisdom about suffering as punishment for sin was no longer sufficient for Job to make sense out of his condition. In the case of Clifford Harris (in *Death Dance: A True Story of Drug Addiction and Redemption*), the window of opportunity came when the conviction that he was an ugly boy was no longer adequate for his new emergent identity. Jefferson's community (in *A Lesson Before Dying*) felt that his recruitment into the identity of an animal was not adequate, and eventually, their convictions presented a window of opportunity for Jefferson to identify with Jesus dying on the cross. Raymond Tyler (in *Abide With Me*) learned to experience himself differently after an encounter with an angel from God, and Basil Henderson (in *If This World Were Mine*) began his transformation process as the pain from his past surfaced at an inconvenient time. Ava Johnson's transformation (in *What Looks Like Crazy on an Ordinary Day*) began when she returned home and began to discover love and vocation. The point is that windows of opportunity come when there are crises, losses, and predictable transitions in life.

When people in need present themselves and the windows of opportunity are open, the pastoral caregiver needs to help these persons understand what is taking place. Some sort of assessment needs to take place.

People need help understanding what is happening. This is the point where reflection on the novels in the first stage of the pastoral theological process becomes helpful. The pastoral caregiver may spend many hours outside of the immediate caregiving situation reflecting on pastoral practice in light of theory and theology. This is done so that the pastoral caregiver has a reservoir of insights from which to draw during the actual caregiving encounter. Perspective conversations developed from reflecting on the novels are helpful when confronting an actual situation. One never knows exactly which insights might be helpful, but this reflective reservoir remains a latent yet available resource from which to draw important insights.

As pastoral caregivers, it is important to help those who come for counseling to identify the conversations that are at work in their life. A model for patterning this process comes from Raymond's encounter with Kyle during the angel scene when Kyle tells Raymond to listen to the snow rather than to the rain. The rain represents those noisy conversations that one hears while growing up and those that are dominant in culture. The snow conversations are those that come from fellowship with God. The role of the pastoral counselor, then, is to help those in need work through the voices of the rain and identify the voice of the snow.

Getting to the voice of the snow is not easy. One has to sort through many conversations and pay attention to the ones into which one has been recruited. Those in need of help and pastoral caregivers must identify the themes and images of these conversations, map the influence that these conversations have had, decide to make changes in these conversations, and finally order these conversations in light of our God conversations.

Significant in the process of revising conversations that have once dominated one's life is the exploration of some of the themes and plots that undergird those conversations. The most significant dimension of sacred identity formation is the reality of how fellowship with God enables us to embrace the suffering we are undergoing for the sake of partnership with God in redeeming the world. Underneath the problems of the world is an unfolding plot where God is redeeming the world. While our culture emphasizes avoiding pain and suffering by whatever means is necessary, fellowship with God teaches us to embrace our suffering as a true sign that transformation of creation is taking place. When we decide to become partners with God in redeeming creation, the forces of evil become more intense. Why God permits this is not known, but we do know that in fellowship with God we can hasten the coming of God's reign. The point is that sacred identity formation and vocation are linked to fellowship with God, and these realities will continue to be present despite the presence of suffering. Our task as pastoral caregivers is to learn to do our caregiving with the resources in partnership with God. We can help those who come for caregiving to realize that privileging God conversation and the benefits that this affords gives us enough resources to live victoriously despite the existence of suffering.